Wishes of Wisdom

Joshua learns about the power of a wish

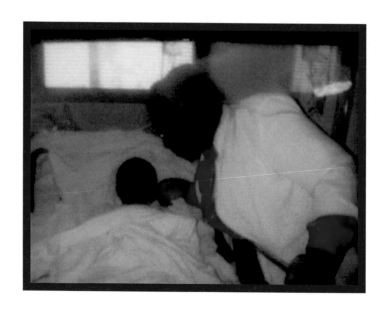

In Loving Memory of My Grandmother

Mildred Wigfall Green
Thank you for your wisdom!
Sincerely your "Macky"

ISBN-10: 0615964753
ISBN-13: 978-0-615-96475-1

Printed in the U.S.A.
Visit: www.misterBinspires.com

Wishes of Wisdom

Joshua

Learns lessons from his wishes

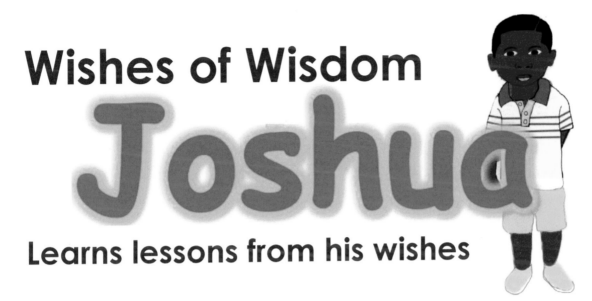

Written and illustrated by:

One dark night
the stars were so bright,
Joshua cried because
something just wasn't right.
He sat on a hill as he remembered
what happened at school.
The children teased him and that
was not cool.
Joshua hated himself and
he continued to cry all night.
Then a ghost appeared to
see if he was alright.

It wasn't a ghost at all......

The ghost was actually
Joshua's fairy grandmother;
whom he loved and missed so much.
She smiled and gave him a big warm touch!

"You are unique;
that means that there is no one else like you.
Many people may look, walk, and talk like you,
but there is only one you.
I searched the world asking
if anyone knew a person like you.
No one had a clue.
Since you wished upon a star,
to be like everyone and everything else,
when you awaken your dream
will finally come true,"
said his fairy grandmother, and away she flew.

As Joshua walked into school,

he couldn't believe his eyes.

Everyone ran from him and he didn't know why.

He touched the door and he saw that

his body was orange, green and blue.

He wished to be cool, and his wish came true!

Joshua became a tree frog with slimy hands.

He could only flop around and not even stand.

MiSTER B, his teacher was the only person

who did not run away.

Instead, he caught Joshua

to teach the class about frogs that day.

Joshua hated being small, so he wished to be tall.

"Poof!"

His wish came true and he didn't have to

worry about that at all.

He wished to be tall and now he

can see over the trees,

but his neck is so long that he has to eat and drink

water on his knees.

His little pink tongue is now long and blue.

Since he's so, so tall, standing in buildings

will be hard to do.

As Joshua looked into the mirror,

he hated that his neck was so very long.

Sadly, his wish had gone all wrong.

He cried, "I wish my neck didn't look like this!"

"Poof!"

Joshua turned into a fish!

Everyone laughed and told jokes

when they saw Joshua come around.

He was not only a fish, but he was also a clown.

He ate worms for breakfast, lunch, and dinner.

He still wasn't satisfied and wished to be slimmer.

"Poof!"

Joshua wished to be slimmer,
so now he is a snake.
He will eat from the ground
without using a plate.
Now he has to walk on his belly,
just to get around.
Instead of words to speak,
he has to make hissing sounds.
He has to eat his food by swallowing it whole.
Joshua should just be himself
so he wouldn't have to live in a hole.

Joshua complained once again,
that he hated being so small.
"Poof!"
He became big and strong,
with a trunk and all!
Now he's an elephant
with big ears and a long nose.
When he talks, he screams
and makes all ears close.
When he walks, everyone will know
that he's on his way.
Be careful what you wish for
and watch what you say.

Joshua wanted to be cool
so everyone would be nice!
"Poof!"
He turned into a cool penguin on floating ice!
You would think that Joshua would learn by now,
to just be himself,
but he made another wish to be someone else.

Joshua was very clever,
he was careful in what he said.
He cried, "I wish I was more like my friend Jake, who
wears a cool hat on his head."

Joshua became Jake and
he was happy as could be;
until he got home
and found out that Jake was allergic
to cheese and macaroni.
He hated being allergic to his favorite dish.
So, he cried to make one last wish!

Then his fairy grandmother appeared.....

"You are unique; that means that there is no one else like you!
Many people may look, walk, and talk like you but there is only one you.
I searched the world asking if anyone knew a person like you.
No one had a clue.
If you wish to be yourself,
when you awaken your wish will finally come true,"
said his fairy grandmother and away she flew.

I wish......

I wish......

I wish......

to be

ME!!!

The End......for now

About the Author and Illustrator
MISTER Anthony Broughton

Hailing proudly from Cross, South Carolina, Mr. Anthony Broughton, affectionately known as "MiSTER B," is an innovative educator and servant leader. He is the author and illustrator of the book Lessons by Nature. Naturally gifted in the creative arts, MiSTER B was always engaged in manifesting his imaginations. He aspires to max out his humanity by using his innate gifts and passion to positively impact the world! He enjoys fashion, creative arts, jogging, traveling, and spending time with family and friends. Be on the look out for more books in the book series Journeys with Joshua: Life Lessons for Little Leaders.

Thanks to my supportive family: The Broughtons, Wigfalls, Nelsons, and Pinckneys of Cross, South Carolina and the Singletons of St. Stephen, South Carolina. Special thanks to Tamara Canzater and Robin McCants (Children's Garden Child Development Center), Christopher Felder, Tracy Powell (McCormick Learning Center), Georgiann Rogers, CROSS ELEMENTARY SCHOOL- DR.CAROLYN GILLENS, PRINCIPAL. "It takes a village to raise a child" –African Proverb

For class visits, bulk orders w/ autographs, conference presentations and more, buzz to Mr. B's beehive at www.misterBinspires.com

Made in the USA
Lexington, KY
21 September 2017

1516

1519 1520 1521

18 February
Katherine
of Aragon
gives birth to
Princess Mary

25 June
The birth of
Henry Fitzroy,
the King's
illegitimate son

7-24 June
Henry holds
peace talks with
Francis I at the
Field of Cloth
of Gold

11 October
Pope Leo X
bestows Henry
with the title
'Defender of
the Faith'

2 May 1519
Leonardo da Vinci
dies in France.
Legend says Francis
I held Leonardo's
head in his arms as
he died

1515
The Vatican appoints
the painter Raphael
chief architect of
St Peter's

1517
Seville Cathedral
is completed after
115 years of
construction

22 September 1520
Suleiman I
succeeds his father
Selim I as Sultan of
the Ottoman Empire

1521
Mexico city is
captured by Hernán
Cortés and claimed
for Spain

1525

1528

18 June
Henry Fitzroy
is created Earl
of Nottingham
and Duke of
Richmond and
Somerset by
King Henry

22 January
Henry VIII
and Francis I
declare war
on Emperor
Charles V
of Spain

24 February 1525
The French are
defeated by the
Habsburgs at the
Battle of Pavia

HENRY VIII ❁ 500 FACTS

Brett Dolman, Suzannah Lipscomb, Lee Prosser,
David Souden and Lucy Worsley

The Field of Cloth of Gold by an unknown artist, *c*1545.

Contents

Henry VIII (detail).
School of Hans Holbein,
c1540-5.

INTRODUCTION

He is the most readily recognised monarch in British history: his shape, his stance, his looks, his glance. His actions five hundred years ago have had an impact upon every person in Britain that lasts to this day. He is King Henry VIII. This book is devoted to understanding the man and his age – and it does so in a novel and entertaining way, in 500 bite-sized chunks that when put together express Henry VIII, his life and times. There is much to dip into and enjoy, there are new things to discover here and surprising links to explore.

What do we know about Henry VIII? Born 1491, became King 1509, died 1547. That he had six wives. And that he liked to have people's heads chopped off.

School children still learn the rhyme that describes the fate of those women he married: divorced, beheaded, died, divorced, beheaded, survived. David Starkey, the leading historian of Henry VIII, writing recently in an essay for the guidebook to Hampton Court Palace, described Henry and his wives as all coming 'straight from central casting. The playboy, the monster, the saint, the schemer, the doormat, the dim fat one, the sexy teen and the swot'.

This man's search for wedded bliss and dynastic stability would alone have made him extraordinary, but there was so much more to the King and his age.

Henry VIII was very tall and always well-built; as a massively overweight older man he cut an even more impressive figure. He was intelligent, with a fine memory, a clear grasp of events and actions, a sharp wit and a highly developed sense of his own self-worth. He was also sports-mad, with a passion for hunting, hawking, jousting, swordplay, tennis and other activities of pleasure and exertion. Music and dance were other passions of his. Henry surrounded himself with bright young men who rode, tumbled and played as hard as he did.

With all this enthusiasm for pleasure, Henry was never very assiduous at attending to business and to matters of state. The routine bored him. He found writing, as he himself expressed it, 'somewhat tedious and painful'. Above all, he was prone to quick-fire likes and dislikes – some were in favour, while others went out of favour, and everybody watched to see where the royal approval lay and as importantly where it would move next. Some have described Henry VIII as being like a spoilt child with a toy, who broke each person he had once loved into pieces when he had grown tired of them. Wives, ministers and courtiers all lived and sometimes died at the royal command.

Henry VIII acted in similar ways on issues and policies. The most striking example is over religion. At the outset he was a pious Catholic who offered the Pope in Rome an unbending loyalty. Henry VIII later earned himself the distinction of being the monarch who brought the Protestant Reformation to England. The break with Rome was political, in order that Henry could divorce his first wife, Katherine of Aragon who had failed to give him a living son and heir. But once the religious genie was let out of the bottle it proved impossible to put it back in. Henry moved progressively in a more Protestant direction, but many around him including his second wife Anne Boleyn and Archbishop Thomas Cranmer moved further and faster.

Allied to this was the biggest land grab the country has ever seen, with the dissolution of religious houses. Smaller monasteries, friaries and convents were the first to go, their land, buildings and treasures seized at royal command in 1536, while the larger and wealthier institutions followed suit four years later. The vast wealth locked up in ecclesiastical institutions was released, with land and buildings transferred into royal hands, redistributed to loyal supporters or sold to the highest bidders. Words that greeted his accession, 'Our King is not after gold, or gems, or precious metals, but virtue, glory, immortality', now rang hollow. In the last years of his life Henry VIII may have been the wealthiest monarch ever to have sat on the throne of England, and he surrounded himself with magnificence and rich display.

This gives a picture of Henry VIII as being capricious and arbitrary. He was certainly both of those things. Yet he was also constrained by the rule of law and guided by exceptionally able ministers. Cardinal Wolsey and then Thomas Cromwell ran the country on behalf of their royal master. Wolsey fell from grace and power in 1529 when he failed to secure the royal divorce. Cromwell was marched to the executioner's block in 1540 in the aftermath of the fiasco of Henry's fourth marriage to the unlovely Anne of Cleves, falling foul of the powerful Howard clan and their supporters on the still-powerful Council that advised the King. And although many went to their deaths at the King's behest, charged with a very broadly-defined treason, they did so under a semblance of law and judicial process. Many of the landmark changes of Henry VIII's reign were made by Acts of Parliament rather than at the royal whim. The need to call parliament, both to raise money and to pass laws, helped further cement its developing role in the process of government.

What was the nation over which Henry ruled? England was for the most part a small player on the European stage, but of growing stature as it acquired international recognition and assumed the leadership of opposition to Rome. Henry VIII's father, Henry VII, had aligned his country to the powerful Spain by arranging for the marriage of Katherine of Aragon to his son Arthur, and then after Prince Arthur's early death,

Prince Henry married the young widow. In a sometimes perplexing series of diplomatic alliances, England's support for other European powers shifted with the balance of power; a few military successes in Europe and in Scotland were celebrated, but the many reverses and defeats were not readily acknowledged.

England was a small nation; although population growth soared from the middle of the 16th century, until that point it was slow or non-existent and numbers were struggling to get back to the 3 million mark they had last reached before the Black Death of 1349. Towns and cities were small, and England was overwhelmingly rural. All the same it was a relatively wealthy nation for its size, principally from the profits of the wool trade – wool rather than cloth, and for export rather than home consumption. The magnificent churches of East Anglia and the West Country from the decades around 1500 are testimony to that wealth, expressed in allegiance to God.

For all the rhetoric about an immoral and stagnant church, used to help justify the Reformation process, it is evident that there was a vigorous piety in England. Some let the old church go without a murmur, but others deeply resented and resisted the changes. The year of greatest crisis for Henry VIII was 1536, when risings in the north and east threatened his regime; the threat was countered partly by force, partly by the strong allegiance of leading families who were tied into the centre by positions at court, money and favour.

One of Henry VII's greatest legacies to his son was the peace and prosperity that accompanied the end of the civil wars of the 15th century. Henry VIII, as himself a product through his parents of both the royal houses of Lancaster and York, benefited from the determined attempts to break the overweening power of the nobility, weaken local loyalties and build up loyalty to the throne. The financial strength of the kingdom in 1509 was another boon to a new king. The peace and prosperity of those with land and wealth was reflected in the houses that they built for themselves, without the need for defences and bringing new architectural pretension to bear. Nowhere was that pretension and grandeur better expressed than in the great houses that were built for Henry VIII, Whitehall Palace, Nonsuch and, the great survivor, Hampton Court Palace among them.

The King is dead, long live the King. For Henry VIII is around us still.

Henry VIII helped to define monarchy, and he embodied it. If he was one of the greatest English monarchs, his second daughter Queen Elizabeth I was arguably of equal importance. His portrait by Holbein established Henry VIII in the public imagination, and he is as recognisable today as he was in the 16th century. At the opening of his reign, England was a minor player on the European dynastic and diplomatic stage; by its close, England had become a power to be reckoned with.

From Charles Laughton to Sid James and Jonathan Rhys Meyers, he has been a plum theatrical part to play. The title Defender of the Faith, given to him by the Pope and then appropriated for a new Protestant outlook, is still held by the Queen and appears on the coinage. Institutions and the wealth stemming from the dissolution of the monasteries, from country houses to City of London institutions and Oxbridge colleges, help form the Establishment. So does the Church of England, the state church that came out of his reign. The Reformation was the greatest and longest-lasting single legacy of Henry VIII's age, and represents as much of a turning point in national life as any other event in the past nine hundred years. In the secular sphere, government departments still occupy the site of Whitehall Palace, Wolsey's legacy to his royal master; Parliament occupies the Palace of Westminster, that Henry VIII deserted after it was partly destroyed by fire; and ambassadors from other countries are presented to the Court of St James, the third of Henry's Westminster palaces. Many of his dozens of other houses and palaces may have perished, but Hampton Court remains (or rather, half of it does) to convey the magnificence of the King and of his reign. All the As – art, architecture, armour – recall Henry VIII.

This is a book that is greater than the sum of its parts. Dip in, and you will find new things, quirky facts and surprising juxtapositions. Put it all together, and it will convey the roller-coaster of love, life and death that was the world of Henry VIII and his age.

Henry VIII (detail).
School of Hans Holbein,
c1540-5.

HENRY THE MAN

'Pastime with good company
I love, and shall until I die…
Hunt, sing and dance,
My heart is set,
All goodly sport
To my comfort
Who shall me let?'

These words and their music are generally attributed to Henry VIII himself, and they sum up the man and the monarch. He loved a good time, and tended to surround himself with those who also enjoyed pleasure and 'good company'. Henry was a big man: his vital statistics are remarkable enough today, and all the more so for an age when people were generally smaller and he would have towered over others. He had a big appetite, for food, later for women, for art and architecture, for horseplay and martial display. All those appetites contributed to his sad decline in later years, taking him from the fit, young, playboy athlete to a bloated and diseased late middle age. The attributes and character of the man translated directly into those of the king and ruler, for with Henry VIII it is never possible to dissolve the links between the two.

Henry as hunk

Henry was tall, and splendidly built. As a young man he was described with admiration by visitors to court. 'Nature could not have done more for him', said one in 1519, before the King's magnificent physique turned to monstrous bulk.

3

At 24, Henry was described as 'the most handsomest potentate I ever set eyes on'. A medal of Henry's profile from c1525 by Lucas Horenbout shows his aquiline nose and strong jaw-line.

4

As a young man, Henry wore his auburn hair in a bob. At 44 he had it cropped close to his head and commanded all men at court to do the same.

5

Henry's eyes were blue, his eyesight good and he was a fine shot, although he wore spectacles in later life.

6

Henry began to wear a beard permanently in 1535, ordering that 'from henceforth his beard… would be knotted and no more shaven'.

7

Henry's lips were very thin.

8

In later life, the King took to walking with a staff, and by 1545, had started using a sort of wheelchair called a 'tramme'. This was probably pulled along by men heaving on ropes. He was also thought to have a form of stairlift that helped him climb stairs at Whitehall Palace.

1

Henry was 1.87m tall (6ft 2in). The average Londoner measured 1.70m (5ft 5in).

2

As a fit, trim 23-year-old, Henry's chest measured 106cm (42in) and his waist 89cm (35in). By age 50 his chest was a massive 144cm (57in) and and his waist a bloated 137cm (54in).

9

Men's calves were considered deeply sexy in the 16th century – and Henry certainly had a fine shapely pair. All the better for dancing!

10

Yuk! Henry's corpse is said to have exploded two weeks after his death on 28 January 1547. Two 19th-century commentators, apparently quoting contemporary documents, say that the lead casing of Henry's coffin burst (or perhaps the coffin fell), putrid matter leaked from it, and stray dogs wandered into St George's Chapel, Windsor and licked up his blood. It's a possibility – after a fortnight, decomposition would have been quite advanced. But the same story is told of other historical figures, including Henry's daughter Elizabeth I.

Copy of Holbein's *Whitehall Mural* (detail) painted in 1667 by Remigius van Leemput. *Left: Henry VIII* by Susanna Horenbout, c1526-7.

*Music and musicians often filled the Tudor palace of Hampton Court,
and Henry VIII himself was a talented composer and performer.*

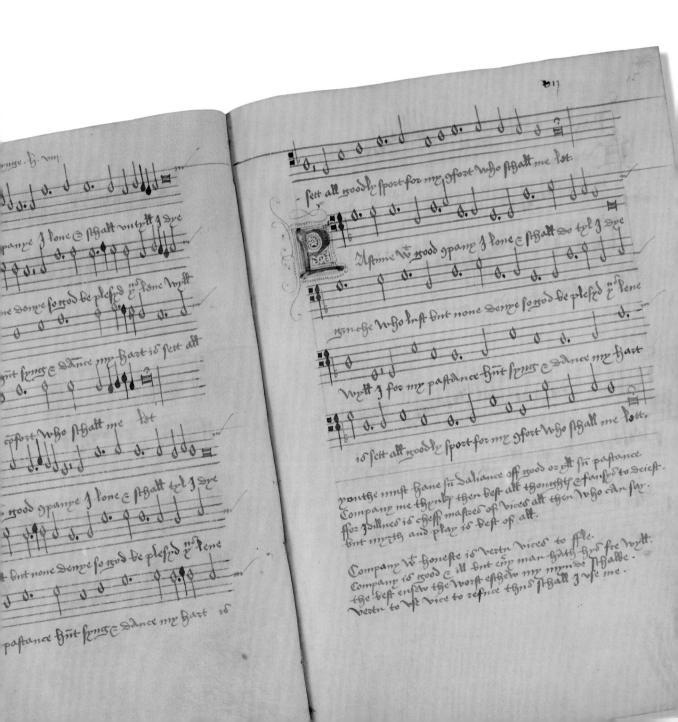

harmonies for a choir of five voices in each case.

15

The songs 'Helas, madame' and 'Pastime with good company' are attributed to Henry VIII. The lyrics reveal a romantic, even soppy side to the King.

> *'Alas, madam,*
> *who I love so much,*
> *Allow me to be your*
> *humble servant,*
> *Your humble servant*
> *I will always remain,*
> *And as long as I live,*
> *no other will I love'*

16

Henry loved a background of music. On occasions, his personal organist would play for the King and court for four hours at a stretch. Dionisio Meo, also known as Dennis Memmo, had been brought to England from St Mark's in Venice in 1516, and was a favourite of Henry's. The King said of him that 'he is the most honest fellow imaginable and one of the dearest,

11

Lutes were a favourite instrument; Henry owned 26, plus a collection of trumpets, viols, rebecs, sackbuts, fifes, drums, harpsichords and organs.

12

Henry's first wife, Katherine of Aragon, had her own consort of four viols, played by Italian musicians. Ambrose and Alexander came from Milan, while Vincent and Albert came from Venice. All earned eightpence for a day's playing.

13

The King himself liked to sing. Two of his favourite songs were 'By the banks and I lay', and 'As I walked the wood so wild'.

14

Henry wrote at least two sets of music for a sung mass. This was a considerable achievement, as he had to compose

for no one has ever served me better or more faithfully'. Henry had many other foreign musicians at court, including trumpeters, flautists and lute players.

17

By 1547, Henry had 60 musicians on his payroll, as well as the singers, Gentlemen and Children of the Chapel Royal.

18

Henry nutured talent for his choir as carefully as a football manager. Once, after a competition between their two chapel choirs, which Thomas Wolsey's won, Henry poached the best singers from the cardinal's choir.

19

The choir of the Chapel Royal had to follow the King as he moved from palace to palace, until 1533 when they settled down at St James's Palace.

20

In 1542, the name Thomas Tallis appears in the list of Gentlemen of Henry VIII's Chapel Royal. One of the greatest English composers of all time, his motet of 40 voices was probably later performed for Elizabeth I's 40th birthday.

Henry as style leader

Henry was described as the 'best-dressed sovereign in the world' by Venetian ambassador Sebastian Giustinian in 1519, who also noted that the King had spent '16,000 ducats for the wardrobe'.

21

Henry's outfits were posh versions of the standard Tudor male costume – a gown, doublet and hose. Henry VIII's gowns were sumptuous. He ordered a total of 79 during his reign; one made in 1537 was 'crimson velvet embroidered all over with damask gold and pearls and stones'.

22

Henry didn't spare the bling when it came to his bonnets! One of his favourites was black velvet, 'garnished with eight great balas [rubies] set in gold and sixteen flowers of gold with four pearls in every flower and a great brooch of gold with a great balas [ruby] and other small diamonds set in it also garnished with five pearls and one great pearl hanging at it'.

23

Hose included the breeches (or 'upperstocks') worn to cover the thigh, which often matched the doublet. Henry VIII particularly liked breeches in the German style, with panes of velvet slashed to show the silk lining, all gathered in at the knee. His codpiece, which was often heavily padded and elaborately decorated, was part of the breeches. Below the knee, Henry wore stockings (or 'netherstocks') made from taffeta, wool, linen, or sometimes silk, which were held up by garters.

From left to right: Henry VIII (detail) by Hans Holbein the Younger, 1536; Henry VIII, School of Hans Holbein, c1540-5; the King's hawking glove and a detail from a portrait of the King, School of Hans Holbein, c1540-5.

24

Next to his skin Henry wore a linen shirt. This could frequently be washed, and was also used for bathing. Henry VIII's shirts, made for him by women including his first wife, Katherine of Aragon, were finely embroidered and decorated.

25

Unlike the average Tudor man, Henry had nightshirts, made of silk.

26

The doublet, worn underneath the gown, fitted to the upper body and often had skirts. Sleeves were sometimes detachable, and fastened at the front with buttons or ties. Henry's doublets were made of velvet or satin, and were richly decorated.

27

Gloves were part of fashionable dress, and were usually made from leather. One of Henry VIII's doe-skin hawking gloves, decorated with (probably) gold thread, survives in the Ashmolean Museum, Oxford.

28

Henry VIII bought a lot of shoes. He also had slippers, boots and buskins (soft, short boots). He even had shoes made to play Tudor-style football, and special hunting boots.

29

Henry frequently wore the insignia of the Order of the Garter, including the garter itself, seen on his left leg *(above)*.

30

On important occasions of state, Henry wore his ceremonial robes, made for him at the time of his coronation in 1509. This fabulous outfit included a show-stopping, floor-length formal mantle with a train, made of gold brocade lined with ermine.

Henry as healer

Henry VIII was a keen amateur apothecary and devised numerous 'plastres', 'balmes', 'waters, lotions and decoctions', many of which were intended to ease the pain and inflammation of the legs that he suffered in later life.

Here are ten of Henry's remedies, with his leg ulcer potion printed in full.

31
A plaster for leg ulcers.

Take a pint of rose oil, plantain water and rose water, two ounces each of myrtle seed and plantain seed, and half an ounce of long worms which have been slit and washed in white wine for two hours. Mix the waters and the worms with the oil, mix in the seeds and warm gently on the fire. Take them off, cover and leave for two days and nights, before boiling again, this time until all the water is gone. Strain them through a fine cloth, then add litharge of gold and white pearl, washed twice in white wine. Then take red coral, rinse it three or four times with plantain water, and add this to the mixture. Stir them well together, boil them over a fire until it becomes plaster-like.

Several of these ingredients have useful properties: plantain promotes healing, and is anti-bacterial, whilst myrtle is still used in homeopathic skincare remedies because of its antiseptic and bactericidal properties. The alcohol in white wine would have cleansed the wound. Gold and pearls, although widely used in early modern medicine, actually have little medicinal worth, and would not have relieved the King's ulcer. Although live maggots can be used to clean wounds, mashed worms would not have relieved Henry's leg. Litharge is a protoxide of lead, made by exposing melted lead to a current of air; it was called litharge of gold when prepared with red lead, and is toxic to humans!

Among the King's other remedies are the following lotions, demonstrating his obsession to cure the pain of his leg:

32

An ointment devised by the King's Majesty at Cawoode to dry sores and comfort the limb, called the sweet ointment.

33

The King's ointment to heal wounds, devised and made at Cawoode.

34

The King's Majesty's ointment to dry sores devised at Fotheringhay and made at Hampton Court.

35

The King's ointment made at St James's to cool and dry and comfort the limb.

36

A russet ointment devised by the King's Majesty at Hampton Court to heal sores. Contained melilot flowers, an emollient.

37

A green ointment devised by the King's Highness to take away heat, and irritation, and to resolve and ease pain.

38

A plaster devised by the King's Majesty to heal painful ulcers.

39

A black plaster devised by the King's Highness.

40

A plaster devised by the King's Highness to resolve, and heal ulcers, and to reduce the heat.

Far left: Illustration from the *Book of Simple Medicines, c*1470. *Above:* Barber-Surgeon's instrument case.

Henry as patient

For the first 35 years of his life, Henry's magnificent body served him well, despite the perils of plague, sweating sickness, dangerous sports and the hazards of Tudor medicine.

41
Henry suffered an attack of smallpox in February 1514.

42
Henry had an attack of malaria in 1521 and occasionally thereafter. It was especially severe in 1541.

43
Henry was prone to headaches, sore throats and catarrh.

44
Henry hurt his left foot playing tennis in 1527 and again in 1529.

45
Henry's greatest accident was in January 1536 when he fell from his horse while jousting. He was unconscious for two hours, and Anne Boleyn blamed her subsequent miscarriage of a male child on the shock at Henry's fall. He was forbidden to joust any more by the Privy Council.

46
Henry had a chronic leg ulcer, first mentioned in 1527-8 but aggravated by his fall in 1536. The ulcer often became inflamed and Henry did not rest long enough for it to heal.

47
Towards the end of his life the overweight King had enormously swollen, dropsical legs, due to chronic heart failure and his obesity.

48
There is no evidence that Henry VIII was syphilitic.

49
Henry appears to have suffered from some form of depression in the second half of his life, with a particularly bad bout in 1541.

50
Like many people, in later life, Henry's eyesight worsened and he needed glasses for reading. His spectacle case was 'of gold engraven with the arms of England'.

Left: Henry VIII jousting.
Below: The King pictured
on his deathbed in
Edward VI and the Pope
by an unknown artist,
c1570.

THE ENDVR
WORDE ATH
OF THE FOR
LORD EVER

SVPERSTITION

ALL FLESHE
IS GRASSE

51

The famous 'Silvered and Engraved'
field armour, 1515, was the first known
product to come out of Henry's
new workshop at Greenwich. It was
decorated to commemorate his
marriage to Katherine of Aragon.

52

In around 1514, Maximilian I presented
Henry VIII with a suit of armour and
an even more fabulously embossed
horse armour, or bard, to go with it.

Henry as warrior

Henry sought to copy previous English kings with success on the battlefield. He spent heavily to equip both himself and his army and navy with the most modern arms and armour. He established the royal armour workshop at Greenwich, London, and commissioned many fabulous pieces.

The embossing, probably done by Fleming Paul van Vrelant, features details from the Order of the Golden Fleece, which Henry was awarded in 1505, and the pomegranate badge of his wife Katherine.

53

A Foot and Combat suit was made in 1520 for Henry to wear at the great tournament, the Field of Cloth of Gold. However, a change in the tournament rules meant that Henry never wore the armour and it was abandoned.

54

This Tonlet armour *(left)* was put together in a very short space of time by the armourers at Greenwich for the King to wear at the Field of Cloth of Gold in 1520. The masterful armourers adapted a number of existing pieces and created this beautiful suit.

Etched decorations include figures of St George, the Virgin and Child and Tudor roses. The amour also reflected Henry's fashion sense; the shape of the breastplate and tonlet (skirt) mimic the jerkin with flaired skirt popular during his reign.

55

A Greenwich field armour, made between 1520 and 1525, was presented by Henry VIII to the Maréchal de Fleuranges after the Field of Cloth of Gold, to reward his valiance in combat with the King.

56

This famous 'horned helmet' (above) is all that remains of a suit of armour given to Henry by Maximilian I in 1514.

57

It is likely that the suit given to Henry by Maximilian was very similar to a highly decorated, fretted armour given to Charles V after the Battle of Tournai in 1514. Henry's armour was apparently melted down as scrap in 1649 after the Civil War, but records show that it too was decorated with silver-gilt panels laid over velvet.

58

Henry had two suits of armour made for him in 1544 for his Boulogne campaign, in which he took part. One, made at Greenwich, was decorated with embossed, etched and gilt scales. Sadly all that remains of this are the crinet (protection for the horse's neck) and the right gauntlet. The whole armour must have created the impression of a huge sea-god!

59

The field and tournament armour pictured *(above)* was made in Greenwich for Henry in 1540. It may have been intended for a tournament held in May that year. However, it's unlikely that Henry's age (49) and great bulk allowed him to participate. The decoration is at least in part by the artist Hans Holbein the Younger, better known for his royal portraits of the Tudor court.

60

The inventory taken at the King's death in 1547 lists a personal collection of weapons including 94 swords, 36 daggers, 15 rapiers, 12 woodknives, 7 crossbows and 100 breech-loading arquebuses (guns). Henry was a gun enthusiast and he encouraged experimentation, looking for weapons with tremendous firepower, but still compact enough to handle.

Far left, and above: Details from Henry's armour for field and tournament, 1540.
Above left: The 'horned helmet' *c*1514.
Left: The Meeting of Henry VIII and the Emperor Maximilian (detail) by an unknown artist, *c*1545.
Right: Knee defences from the 1540 armour.

61

Henry spent many hours hawking, and after his death his private apartments were found to be full of falconry equipment. Once, in his thirties, he was nearly killed pursuing his hawk when he fell headfirst into a ditch of muddy water. A footman saved the dazed King from drowning.

62

Henry had a good ear, and a fine voice.

63

Well-known for 'dancing magnificently in the French style', and performing 'wonders and leaps like a stag', Henry could dance all night and still be fresh and 'wonderfully merry' the next day.

64

Henry was a strong – and usually victorious – wrestler. However, to his fury he was defeated in a royal bout with Francis I at the Field of Cloth of Gold in 1520.

65

Henry was very musical, and contemporaries describe him as 'Playing at the recorders, flute and virginals'. He also composed many tunes that celebrated his favourite activities: hunting, singing and dancing and all 'goodly sport'.

66

Henry loved a good game of football, commissioning a pair of football boots at a cost of 4 shillings (about £100 today). Tudor football, in which you could pick up and throw the ball, like modern-day rugby, could be a violent game with no limit to the number of players on each side. The game eventually became so violent that it was banned.

67

For many years Henry VIII was one of the best jousters in England and, despite the risks and suffering from a number of injuries and narrow escapes, it was said that he had 'no respect or fear of anyone in the world'.

Henry as playboy

Henry was sport-mad as a young man and played hard both indoors and out. 'Above the usual height' and 'with an extremely fine calf' to his leg, his favourite pastimes ranged from jousting to singing.

Left: Henry VIII at the Westminster Tournament, 1511.
Below left: Henry VIII Playing the Harp from the *Psalter of Henry VIII*, 1530-47.
Below: A Tudor tennis ball made of leather and hair found at Whitehall.
Below right: A herd of fallow deer grazing in Home Park, Hampton Court.

68

Henry was a particularly keen player of real tennis – so much so that he had courts built at many of his palaces, including Hampton Court. He cut quite a dash, described by an ambassador 'it is the prettiest thing in the world to see him play, his fair skin glowing through a shirt of the finest texture'.

69

The King lost hundreds of pounds to his courtiers through gambling. In his youth he was 'much enticed to play at tennis and at dice, which appetite, certain crafty persons about him perceiving, brought in Frenchmen and Lombards, to make wagers with him, and so he lost much money'.

70

The young King loved to hunt all day, but in later years he avoided an arduous chase by having stags chased towards him so he could pick them off one by one. In one day's hunt in 1541, he and his courtiers shot 200 deer. The herd at Hampton Court today are descendants from Henry's original stock.

Henry as lover

Despite Henry's reputation for womanizing (mainly constructed from films and TV series of the 21st century), we know of only three mistresses, possibly four. He had several near misses too!

Mistresses

71
Elizabeth Blount

Elizabeth (Bessie) Blount was a maid to Queen Katherine of Aragon. Bessie was a great beauty, and in 1519 bore Henry VIII a son – Henry Fitzroy (meaning 'illegitimate King's son'). He later became Duke of Richmond.

72
Mary Boleyn

Henry also had a brief affair with 'The Other Boleyn Girl' Mary, sister to Anne, during the 1520s.

73
Mrs Shelton
While Anne Boleyn was still Queen, a 'Mrs Shelton' – Anne's first cousin – became Henry's mistress for about six months before Jane Seymour caught his eye. Whether this refers to Margaret Shelton or her sister Mary is uncertain.

74
Elizabeth Howard
Anne and Mary Boleyn's mother, Elizabeth Howard, royal lady-in-waiting, was said to have once been the King's mistress. This rumour was hotly denied by Henry himself, who reportedly said 'Never with the mother!' when it was suggested that he had slept with all three women.

The ones that got away
Many possible wives were considered after Jane Seymour's death:

75
Marie de Guise
Henry declared himself very keen on Marie de Guise, daughter of the French Duc de Guise, as she was 'big in person' and he needed an impressive wife. Marie remained unmoved. 'I might be big in person', she later commented, 'but my neck is small'. She married James V of Scotland and became the mother of Mary, Queen of Scots.

76
Louise de Guise
The French offered the beautiful Louise, sister to Marie (above) as second choice but the King considered her for only the briefest moment. The ambassador tempted the King with tales of her beauty and virginity.

77
Marie de Vendome
Marie was another French lovely briefly in the running for the King's attention. Henry may have seen a portrait of her, but he was not satisfied. He wanted her to come to Calais so a selection could be made.

78
Anne of Lorraine
Henry couldn't decide between Louise, Marie and Anne of Lorraine, another French beauty. He suggested to the French ambassador that the lovely ladies be brought to Calais so that he may 'see them and know them some time before deciding'. Horrified, the French ambassador spluttered 'Maybe your grace would like to mount them one after the other and keep the one you find to be the best broken in!'

79
Christina of Denmark
The second daughter of deposed

Danish King Christian II and niece of the Holy Roman Emperor, Charles V, Christina was also suggested as a bride for Henry after her husband the Duke of Milan had died. Henry was very taken with a portrait of her by Hans Holbein, and the English ambassdor was sent to Milan on a marriage mission. Christina was not keen, demonstrating a lively wit when (it is claimed) she replied to the ambassador that if she had two heads then 'one of them would be at the King of England's disposal'.

80
Amelia of Cleves
Amelia was Anne's younger sister. Both sisters were in the running to be Henry's fourth wife at one stage, and both were painted by Hans Holbein in 1539. After much deliberation Henry chose Anne as she was more mature (she was all of 24 compared to Amelia's 22) and so more suitable for a man in his late forties.

Henry overheard

Some of the most exciting documents from the Tudor age record Henry VIII's very words. Here are some snippets of conversations overheard.

Left to right: Bust of a child possibly Henry VIII as a boy by Guido Mazzoni, *c*1498; *The Battle of Pavia* (detail) by an unknown artist, *c*1530; Princess Mary (detail) by Master John, 1544.

'Who wrote this letter? I ask peace of the king of France, who dare not look at me, let alone make war?'

81
Henry is tongue-tied

As a young prince, Henry was rarely heard to speak in public, except to answer a question from his father. According to his biographer J J Scarisbrick, after Henry's elder brother Arthur died, the new and doubly precious heir to the throne was kept under strict supervision, away from the court. No one dared to approach the young Henry or speak to him.

82
Henry is offended

In the summer of 1509, a messenger arrived from France to give thanks for a friendly letter supposedly sent by Henry VIII to the French king. Henry VIII denied all knowledge. He roared: 'Who wrote this letter? I ask peace of the king of France, who dare not look at me, let alone make war?' Then he 'rose and would hear no more'.

'All the enemies of England are gone! Give him more wine'

'We are both young. If it was a daughter this time, by the grace of God the sons will follow'

'Let every man have his doctor. This is mine'

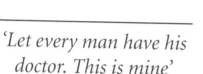

83
Henry is magnanimous
In 1513, John Colet, Dean of Westminster, changed his mind and supported Henry VIII's war on the French. Henry VIII toasted him with a glass of wine and commented: 'Let every man have his doctor. This is mine'.

84
Henry triumphant
A messenger came into Henry VIII's bedchamber in the early hours of 9 March 1525 to tell him the good news that the French had been defeated at the Battle of Pavia. Henry called for a celebratory drink, saying 'All the enemies of England are gone! Give him more wine'.

85
Henry philosophical
In 1516 Henry's first wife, Katherine of Aragon gave birth to a daughter, Mary. Her gender was obviously a disappointment to the King, but at that stage he was still optimistic, reassuring Katherine: 'We are both young. If it was a daughter this time, by the grace of God the sons will follow'. Sadly for Katherine they did not. She seems to have miscarried in the autumn of 1517, then in the following year had yet another stillborn baby. This was her last pregnancy.

'I tell thee it is mine'

86
Henry is jealous

The King was not alone in his pursuit of Anne Boleyn. One of his courtiers, Sir Thomas Wyatt, was also keen. During what must have been a rather tense game of bowls with Wyatt in the late 1520s, a dispute arose over who had won the round. Anne had given Henry a ring that he wore on his little finger, which he now used to point to the winning ball, saying, 'I tell thee it is mine'. Wyatt grasped at once that the King was claiming Anne as well as the point, so he in his turn used a locket on a chain – that Anne had given him – to measure the distance between the balls. Henry understood perfectly and left in a huff.

'If I were to marry again [and] if that marriage might be good, I would surely choose her above all women... These be the sores that vex my mind, these be the pangs that trouble my conscience and for these griefs I seek a remedy'

87
Henry in a tight spot

Called in 1528 to defend his decision to have his marriage to the popular Katherine of Aragon annulled, Henry adopted a regretful public line, explaining his fears that the marriage was not legal (rather than admitting he was desperate for an heir and had fallen in love with Anne Boleyn!). He told a group of dignitaries: 'If I were to marry again [and] if that marriage might be good, I would surely choose her above all women'. He claimed he could simply no longer tolerate living in sin: 'These be the sores that vex my mind, these be the pangs that trouble my conscience and for these griefs I seek a remedy'.

'Am I not a man, a man like any other?'

88
Henry is only human

Soon after Henry's marriage to Anne Boleyn, one of the foreign ambassadors at court made the mistake of suggesting that he might never have any more children. The King exploded with rage: 'Am I not a man, a man like any other?' he yelled in answer to this slur on his potency.

> *'My lord, if it were not to satisfy the world and my realm, I would not do that I must do this day for none earthly thing'*

> *'I will first take a little sleep, and then, as I feel myself, I will advise upon the matter'*

89
Henry does his duty
By the time Anne of Cleves arrived in England in 1540 Henry had gone off the whole idea of marriage. He didn't find Anne attractive, was already interested in Catherine Howard, and the political situation in Europe had changed, so he no longer needed a useful alliance. But it was too late to get out of it. He snarled to Thomas Cromwell on his wedding day: 'My lord, if it were not to satisfy the world and my realm, I would not do that I must do this day for none earthly thing'.

90
Henry's last words
Henry VIII's final recorded words were on the subject of which priest should attend him to administer the last rites. On 27 January 1547 Henry wanted Cranmer to do it, but no great rush. He murmured: 'I will first take a little sleep, and then, as I feel myself, I will advise upon the matter'. When he woke up, in the early hours of 28 January, Cranmer was there, but the King had lost the power of speech, and had to show a sign of his faith by squeezing Cranmer's hand.

Left to right: Anne Boleyn; *Thomas Cromwell* (detail) after Hans Holbein the Younger; *Henry VIII and the Barber-Surgeons* (detail) by Hans Holbein the Younger, 1540; *Edward VI and the Pope* (detail) by an unknown artist, *c*1570.

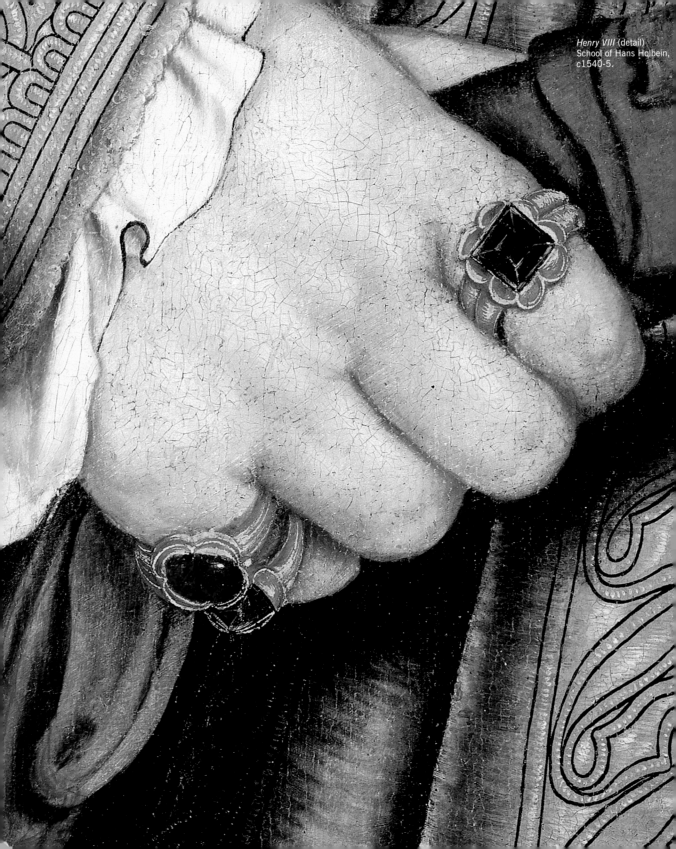

Henry The Husband

❀

The one thing everybody knows about Henry VIII is that he was married many times, more often than any other English monarch. This has given him something of a reputation as a superb lover, and also as a great philanderer. When the huge suit of Henry's foot armour was on open display at the Tower of London from the 19th century, its proud codpiece was worn smooth by the hands of passing women touching it for luck. Not that Henry had much luck in that area himself – the search for a wife and companion was also the search to secure his dynasty with a son and heir (and preferably with a spare). One by one his wives were cast aside, the victims both of their unfortunate fertility histories and of the intrigues at court that meant marriageable young virgins were sacrificed on the marital altar of political and dynastic expedience.

Katherine of Aragon (married 1509-33)

Henry was married to Katherine for almost 24 years. This fact of history still astonishes. Before the years of Henry's aggressive matrimonial consumption, the pair were a happy couple, a united family and a political team.

'Humble and loyal'

91

By marrying Katherine, Henry made a useful political alliance with Katherine's powerful parents. Isabella of Castile and Ferdinand of Aragon were an astonishing couple of huge importance in 16th-century Europe and beyond, who united Spain under their joint crowns.

92

Henry loved Katherine. He married her because he wanted to (although having her father as an ally against the French helped too).

93

Katherine was fair-skinned, with reddish-gold hair, and an oval face. 'There was nothing wanting in her that the most beautiful girl should have', wrote Thomas More, a little sycophantically. On the other hand, she was rather short.

94

As partners they were well-matched. Henry and Katherine shared a similar education and piety, loved finery and display, rode and hunted together. They were young, optimistic, and politically astute.

95

They had a daughter togther. Mary was born in 1516 at Greenwich Palace. Henry doted on his daughter and was extremely proud of her. Katherine took an active role in her education and corrected her Latin homework. They were a family.

96

Katherine was a humanist and scholar, with an enthusiasm for theology (just like Henry). She became the patron of a number of important thinkers, and Erasmus praised her learning.

97

The King left his wife in charge of the country in 1513 when he went to war against France. He trusted her with the Regency and the defence of the realm against France's ally, Scotland.

98

Sady, Henry and Katherine lost at least five children together, with only Mary surviving beyond infancy.

99

Desperate for a male heir (and with Anne Boleyn in his sights) Henry began to want out. He became obsessed with whether Katherine's previous marriage to his brother Arthur had been consumated, which Katherine continued to deny. This became hugely important to Henry as it explained (in his view) why their marriage had not been blessed by God. Katherine had to go.

100

Katherine refused to go quietly. The marriage had failed, ultimately, only because she could not provide Henry with the male heir that his dynastic desire demanded. After a long and messy annulment trial she was dismissed from court. Her last letter to Henry read 'Mine eyes desire you above all things.' She still signed it Katherine the Queen. She died, aged 50, in 1536.

Katherine of Aragon
by an unknown artist,
*c*1530.
Left: The Queen's
badge.

ANNA BOLINA VXOR— HENRI· OCT

Copy of a presumed lost
portrait of Anne Boleyn,
late 16th century.
Right: The Queen's
badge.

Anne Boleyn (married 1533, executed 1536)

Anne was part of an important aristocratic family, the Howards. Her father, who rose on his daughter's success, was Sir Thomas Boleyn. Anne's uncle, Sir Thomas Howard, was the most powerful nobleman in the land.

'The most happy'

101

Henry first spotted Anne in 1526, while she was Queen Katherine of Aragon's lady-in-waiting.

102

She was a glamorous addition to Henry's court, having been educated in France at the courts of Henry's sister Mary, and the new French queen, Claude. Anne spoke French and Latin, wore French styles and was talented at singing and dancing.

103

Anne was seen by some as a key – and unwelcome – influence on the King. Wolsey called her 'the night crow' – cawing into Henry's ear in the intimacy of night.

104

Anne's motto was 'the most happy'. Her badge was a crowned white falcon on a dead branch that burst into Tudor roses.

105

Henry married Anne twice – once secretly in November 1532, and once officially in January 1533. Both were bigamous marriages, as Henry's marriage to Katherine was not annulled until May 1533.

106

Henry VIII and Anne had a child together – Elizabeth was born on 7 September 1533.

107

Anne was evangelical or Protestant in her beliefs, and devout. Her patronage helped advance important religious reformers, such as Matthew Parker, who was to be Archbishop of Canterbury under her daughter Elizabeth. She was also an important supporter of the arts.

108

Henry's second wife was unpopular in the country as a whole. During her coronation procession one observer said that onlookers 'showed themselves as sorry as though it had been a funeral'. On 11 February 1535, a Margaret Chanseler of Suffolk confessed before justices that she had called the Queen a 'goggle-eyed whore'.

109

Henry and Anne had no more live children. In April 1534, reports of Anne's 'goodly belly' hinted she was pregnant, but no miscarriage was ever recorded, which suggested she suffered a phantom pregnancy. Three years later Anne miscarried a much-longed-for male child at three and a half months, on the same day that Katherine of Aragon was buried, 29 January 1536.

110

Henry ordered Anne's execution after she was accused and found guilty of adultery, incest and high treason. This took place at the Tower of London on 19 May 1536, but the King showed her a 'mercy'. At her request, Anne was beheaded cleanly with a sword, not an axe, according to the French custom. On the day of her execution, she comforted herself by saying, 'I heard say the executioner was very good, and I have a little neck', and then laughed heartily.

Jane Seymour (married 1536, died 1537)

Jane may not have lasted long as Henry's third wife, but she gave him what he most desired – a son. She also launched the Seymour family on to the centre stage of Tudor court politics. They never looked back.

'Bound to obey and serve'

111

Jane's looks were not her strong point. The Spanish ambassador described her 'of middle stature and no great beauty'; he also wondered about her virtue, or whether she'd already attracted Henry's attentions because of her talent in bed.

112

Whatever Henry saw in Jane, she provided him with the thing he most desired: a son. Prince Edward was born at Hampton Court in the early hours of 12 October 1537.

113

Jane achieved iconic status during Henry's time. She was immortalised as a young Tudor rose, his favourite queen. Her portrait appeared in paintings after her death and her badges continued to adorn palace walls even after he had married Anne of Cleves.

114

Henry showered Jane with jewellery and gifts. A list of Jane's jewels survives at the British Library, and designs for some of the most elaborate, with Henry and Jane's initials entwined together, can be found at the British Museum.

115

The only surviving portrait we know to have been made of Jane during her lifetime was painted by Hans Holbein. He also designed jewellery and a very beautiful gem-studded cup that Henry gave to his favourite queen.

116

Henry's naughty in-laws created problems for the King. The Seymours were an old prosperous family but an obscure one. The ultimate royal connection changed all that, and their ambition knew no bounds. Both Jane's brothers would eventually be executed for treason, and their descendants were often getting into trouble for arranging secret marriages with princesses, without royal permission.

117

Henry VIII apparently wrote to Jane when he was still married to Anne Boleyn, though his letters have not survived. One was transcribed before it disappeared: Henry styled himself Jane's 'entirely devoted servant'. The letter ended, 'Hoping shortly to receive you in these arms…'

118

Jane's own reputation has fluctuated over the years from 'innocent victim of Henry's dynastic quest', powerless to resist the King's advances, to a capricious schemer who encouraged him. The truth is probably somewhere in the middle, although Henry and Jane were married with indecent haste – 11 days after Anne's execution.

119

While staying out of debates at court, unlike Anne Boleyn, Jane still provided a direct route to the King. So courtiers flocked around her, aware that she provided a new conduit for ambition away from the traditional court families like the Howards.

120

Jane did not survive to see their son grow up. Being queen did not save her from a fate common to many 16th-century women. She died of postnatal complications 12 days after his birth, aged only 28.

Jane Seymour by Hans Holbein the Younger, *c*1536.
Left: The Queen's badge.

Anne of Cleves (married January 1540, divorced July 1540)

Everyone thinks of Anne of Cleves as ugly, stupid and unwanted. It seems incredible that she was even considered as a suitable bride for Henry. But, as ever, the truth is actually more interesting than the fiction…

'God send me well to keep'

121
Marrying Anne of Cleves brought Henry political support in Europe. Henry craved magnificence and recognition, and his ministers were under constant pressure to divert his ambitions into realistic policies. Thomas Cromwell persuaded the King to court the German Duke of Cleves in an attempt to gain more clout in Europe. The Duke's daughters Anne and Amelia were offered up as bait for the widowed King Henry.

122
Henry didn't like having his wives selected for him. He rather preferred his own methods. When one ambassador rather sarcastically suggested parading some of the more eligible prospects naked in front of him, Henry thought this a rather good idea. Certainly, Anne was the only wife Henry was not able to court directly.

123
Even before Anne of Cleves was delivered to England, Henry may have decided he wanted to marry Catherine Howard instead.

124
This portrait of Anne *(opposite)* by Holbein, has inspired painters for centuries, including Degas. It is said to have idealised Anne to such an extent that Henry fell in love there and then, only to be bitterly disappointed when the real woman turned up.

125
The famous story (see above) is probably not true! It became fashionable to criticise Anne over the years, and she only became known as 'the Flanders mare' in the 17th century. However, in reality the political motivation for marrying Anne had receded by the time she arrived in England, and Henry suspected she was secretly engaged to a European prince.

126
Henry and Anne were married in January 1540 but the marriage was annulled six months later.

127
Henry invented a whole string of rather unpleasant excuses to get out of the marriage. Anne had been engaged before (and was therefore 'spoiled'), or she was too naïve. Some, eager to jump on the bandwagon, quite possibly claimed that she was not fit for educated English society.

128
Henry may have grown to like Anne, particularly after his initial infatuation with Catherine Howard had passed. Both Anne and Catherine danced together at Hampton Court over the Christmas festivities of 1541, and there was even gossip at court that Henry had got Anne pregnant.

129
Life wasn't all grim for Anne. She had a parrot, of whom she was very fond. She seems to have been given it as a present in Calais, while she was waiting to travel to England. The household accounts record it travelling from palace to palace.

130
Rumours spread that Henry and Anne, although once married, had committed adultery. This resulted in an angry published denial known as the Remonstrance of Anne of Cleves, nobody knows who wrote it. The rumours went away, Henry turned his attentions elsewhere and Anne retreated into divorced obscurity.

Catherine Howard (married 1540, executed 1542)

Henry was 49, increasingly unwell, overweight and probably feeling his age. Catherine was a pretty teenager, saucy and full of life. Was their marriage doomed from the start?

'No other will but his'

131
Flirtatious Catherine attracted Henry's attention when she was a maid of honour to Anne of Cleves in late 1539. She was the daughter of Lord Edmund Howard and Jocasta Legh, who died when Catherine was very young, so she was brought up by her father's stepmother, the Dowager Duchess of Norfolk.

132
Henry was unaware that his bride-to-be had enjoyed several previous relationships with men. It seems likely Catherine had a romantic liaison with her music teacher Henry Manox (although he later swore they had not had sex), and an affair with Francis Dereham.

133
Henry married Catherine at Oatlands Palace on 28 July 1540, just three weeks after his union to Anne of Cleves was annulled.

134
The young Queen found the role of stepmother hard. Possibly feeling insecure, she soon quarrelled with her stepdaughter, Princess Mary.

135
Besotted, Henry was vulnerable to Catherine's persuasive power. She successfully pleaded with the King for pardon and patronage on behalf of others, including Sir Thomas Wyatt and his associates, charged with treason.

136
It seems likely that Queen Catherine did entertain a Gentleman of the King's Privy Chamber named Thomas Culpeper, with the help of her maid, Jane Boleyn, Lady Rochford, widow of George Boleyn. A letter, used as evidence of her adultery, survives today. In it, she writes to Thomas that her eyes desire to see him above all things, and signs off 'yours as long as life endures'.

137
Henry learnt of Catherine's infidelities and premarital behaviour at Hampton Court on 2 November 1541. A series of informants brought news of Catherine's activities to Archbishop Cranmer. It's thought the Archbishop left a written statement on the King's pew in the Chapel Royal. After confirming the allegations, Henry left Catherine on 6 November, ordered her arrest, and never saw her again.

138
Henry reacted with tremendous sorrow and rage. In a letter to Sir William Paget, the resident ambassador in France, the Privy Council reported that at first Henry was so choked up with emotion that he could not speak, but had finally released 'plenty of tears'.

139
On 10 February 1542 Catherine was taken by barge to the Tower of London, passing under the rotting heads of Culpeper and Dereham displayed on London Bridge. Three days later, on 13 February, she was beheaded, closely followed to the block by Lady Rochford, her accomplice.

140
It is said that Catherine's ghost haunts Hampton Court Palace, her screams echoing down what is known today as 'The Haunted Gallery', where she is supposed to have run to plead with Henry VIII. Many a visitor has felt a thrilling tremble and a chill in this part of the palace!

Portrait of a lady thought to be Catherine Howard, by a follower of Hans Holbein the Younger.
Left: The Queen's badge.

Kateryn Parr (detail) attributed to Master John, *c*1545.
Right: The Queen's badge.

Kateryn Parr (married 1543-7)

Henry's last wife Kateryn was the only one to survive him. She was by all accounts a kind, sensible woman, loving stepmother to his three children and a support to the ageing King.

'To be useful in all I do'

141

At 52, Henry was probably looking for a stable, caring companion. Kateryn Parr was 30, but in no way an 'old maid', even though she had been previously married twice. She was in fact younger than Anne Boleyn had been when she married Henry a decade earlier.

142

Kateryn's parents were Sir Thomas Parr of Kendal, Westmorland and Maud Green. She met Henry in the winter of 1542-3 when she became a lady in the household of Henry's daughter, Princess Mary.

143

Apart from one example of her signature as a child, she always signed her name 'Kateryn Parr KP'. She was named after Katherine of Aragon, Henry's first wife, who probably acted as her godmother!

144

Kateryn was more beautiful than was previously thought, as portraits identified in the mid-2000s show. She had red hair and grey eyes, and was lively and energetic. She loved luxurious fabrics (crimson was her favourite colour), fine perfumes and jewels. Her privy wardrobe accounts even record that she bought a black silk nightgown!

145

Henry VIII was her third husband. Kateryn was married four times, first to Edward Borough of Gainsborough. After four years Edward died and Kateryn married John Neville, Lord Latimer, of Snape Castle in Yorkshire, in 1534. They were married for nine years. Four months after his death, she married Henry VIII in the Queen's Closet at Hampton Court. Within months of burying the King, Kateryn married for a final time to Sir Thomas Seymour.

146

Kateryn was in love with the handsome, charismatic Sir Thomas Seymour before she married Henry.

147

Henry relied on Kateryn to run the country during his absence at war in France in 1544. This strong-willed, intelligent and outspoken woman assumed the role of Queen Regent-General of England and signed five royal proclamations during these months.

148

Princess Elizabeth seems to have been very fond of Kateryn. Of the five surviving letters Elizabeth wrote before she was 16, four are to Kateryn. After Henry VIII's death, Kateryn took custody of the 14-year-old Elizabeth. Her example of female leadership shaped the young Elizabeth's ideas.

149

Kateryn was a vigorous supporter of the English Reformation.

150

Kateryn was the first Queen of England to write and publish her own books and the first Englishwoman to publish a work of prose in the 16th century. She was also an active patron of the arts, supporting artists and artisans.

Letters to wives and soon-to-be wives

Henry's letters to Anne Boleyn survive in the Vatican library, but Henry's from his future queen have vanished. Perhaps he destroyed them when his love turned sour. Tantalising glimpses of his relationships with three other wives also survive.

151
To Anne Boleyn

'My mistress and friend, I and my heart put ourselves in your hands, begging you to recommend us to your good grace and not to let absence lessen your affection…
Your loyal servant and friend'

H Rex

152
To Anne Boleyn

'In debating with myself the contents of your letters I have been put to a great agony; not knowing how to understand them… I beseech you now… to let me know your whole mind as to the love between us… having been for more than a year now struck by the dart of love, and… If it pleases you to do the duty of a true, loyal mistress and friend, and to give yourself body and heart to me… I promise you that not only the name will be due to you, but also to take you as my sole mistress, casting off all others than yourself out of mind and affection, and to serve you only… Written by the hand of him who would willingly remain yours'

HR

153
To Anne Boleyn

'For a present so beautiful that nothing could be more so… I thank you very cordially… for the handsome diamond and the ship in which the lonely damsel is tossed about… assuring you that henceforward my heart shall be dedicated to you alone, with a strong desire that my body could be also thus dedicated… Your loyal and most assured servant'

H seeks AB no other R

154
To Anne Boleyn

'The legate which we most desired arrived at Paris on Sunday or Monday last past so… I trust within a while… to enjoy that which I have so long longed for to God's pleasure and our both comfort… written after the killing of an hart at 11 of the clock, minding with God's grace tomorrow mightily timely to kill another; by the hand of him which I trust shortly shall be yours'

Henry R

(Written on the arrrival of the papal legate to Paris, when Henry hoped his marriage to Katherine of Aragon would be dissolved).

155
To Anne Boleyn

'The cause of my writing at this time (good sweetheart) is only to understand of your good health and prosperity… and seeing my darling is absent I… send her some flesh representing my name; which is hart flesh for Henry'

HR

Letter from Henry VIII to Anne Boleyn.

156
To Anne Boleyn

'I send by this messenger a buck, killed very late yesterday evening by my own hand; hoping that when you eat it, it will remind you of the hunter… Written by the hand of your servant, who often wishes you here instead of your brother'

H Rex

157
To Anne Boleyn

'My dear sweetheart, this is to inform you of the great loneliness that I find here since your departure… wishing myself especially of an evening in my sweetheart's arms, whose pretty breasts I trust shortly to kiss. Written by the hand that was, is, and shall be yours by his will'

HR

158
To Jane Seymour

'My dear friend and mistress, The bearer of these few lines from thy entirely devoted servant will deliver into thy fair hands a token of my true affection for thee… Advertising you that there is a ballad made lately of great derision against me, which… I pray you pay no matter of regard to it. I am not at present informed who is the setter forth of this malignant writing, but if he is found he shall be straightly punished for it… Thus hoping shortly to receive you in these arms I end for the present your own loving servant and Sovereign'

HR

159
To Anne of Cleves

'Right dear and right entirely beloved sister, By the relation of the lord Master, lord Privy Seal and others of our Council… we perceive the continuance of your conformity… and, continuing your conformity, you shall find in us a perfect friend, content to repute you as our dearest sister. We shall, within five or six days, when our Parliament ends, determine your state… minding to endow you with £4000 of yearly revenue. We have appointed you two houses, that at Richmond where you now lie, and the other at Blechinglegh… Be quiet and merry. Thus subscribed, Your loving brother and friend'

HR

(Written to Anne on the day their marriage was annulled. Henry held her in high esteem, saying she would henceforth be known as his 'sister')
12 July 1540.

160
To Kateryn Parr

'The closing up of these our Letters… the castle forenamed with the Dyke is at our comment, and not like to be recovered by the Frenchmen again, as we trust… that the castle and town shall shortly follow the same trade; for as this day… the 8th day of September, we begin three batteries, and have three mines going, by said one which hath done his execution in shaking and tearing off one of their greatest bulwarks… we pray you to give in our name our hearty blessings to all… Written with the hand of your loving husband'

Henry R

(Written before the Battle of Boulogne)
8 September 1544.

Henry The Father

Henry VIII was, by all accounts, a romantic man even if cruelty often overcame the romance. He was also, by those accounts, an attentive and loving father. His two daughters as well as his son were very well taught and were brought up to be scholarly and accomplished. The hope that was invested in a boy almost resulted in Henry making his illegitimate son into his legitimate heir, although the boy's death and the birth of Prince Edward removed that essentially distasteful move. The princesses Mary and Elizabeth were loved, ostracized and reconciled in their turn as a reaction to the fates of their own mothers and of succeeding royal wives.

Prince Edward

Henry VIII had already been the father of no less than nine legitimate children (and an unknown number of illegitimate children!) before Edward was born; yet all of them were either miscarried, died young, or female.

161

Henry's only male heir was born on 12 October 1537 at Hampton Court Palace. His mother Jane Seymour probably gave birth in the same room that Katherine of Aragon had used previously, overlooking Clock Court.

162

Henry had Edward christened three days later. The ceremony took place at Hampton Court Palace, with a huge procession along the galleries to the Chapel. The baby was wrapped in a fur-trimmed robe and carried under a rich canopy borne by four Gentlemen of the King's Privy Chamber. The procession included princesses Mary and Elizabeth.

163

To his enormous sorrow, Henry's third wife died soon after Edward's birth, probably of puerperal fever. Henry 'retired to a solitary place to pass his sorrows', and her funeral took place in the Chapel at Hampton Court very soon after their son's christening.

164

Unlike his father, Edward was not a healthy boy. Royal doctors feared the young prince was 'not of constitution to live long', and they were right. He suffered from grave illnesses such as quartan fever in his childhood, and was to die of bronchopneumonia at the age of 15.

165

Edward owned animals, as did his father. The little prince even had his own fighting bears. In one portrait of Edward at the age of 6, he is shown holding a monkey (perhaps one of those that belonged to Will Somers, his father's fool, or court entertainer).

166

Nothing was too grand for Henry's son. For Christmas 1544, Edward's stepmother Kateryn Parr ordered the 7-year-old Prince a new outfit, of a doublet and coat of crimson velvet with gilt buttons and gold braid, and a velvet cap with a feather. Edward also had his own extensive household, even as a baby.

167

Henry's children did not live together, until Kateryn Parr united them for the first time in an attempt to create family harmony. An enlightened stepmother, she also brought in impressive Latin tutors for Edward and his sisters.

168

In 1542, Henry considered arranging Edward's marriage to the infant Mary, future Queen of Scots. This would have united both branches of the Tudor family and England and Scotland. The engagement was never made, and Edward died before he could marry.

169

Henry's will was fiercely contested. His heir Edward was, at 9, too young to rule so there was a council of regency until he grew up. It appears that someone tinkered with Henry's will (which was unsigned) in favour of the Seymour family, who were to dominate Edward's early reign.

170

Edward's protector was at first his uncle, Edward Seymour, the Duke of Somerset, until he was deposed in 1550. Edward coolly records his execution as a traitor in January 1552: 'the duke… had his head cut off upon Tower hill, between eight and nine o'clock in the morning'.

A portrait of *The Young Edward VI* by Hans Holbein the Younger, c1539.
Left: Prince Edward's christening procession.

PARVVLE PATRISSA, PATRIÆ VIRTVTIS ET HÆRES
ESTO, NIHIL MAIVS MAXIMVS ORBIS HABET.

ANNO DNI · 1 · 5 · 4 ·

Princess Mary by
Master John, 1544.

LADI MARI   DOVGHTER
THE MOST   VERTVOVS PRI
KING HENRI   THE EIGHT

THE AGE OF   XXVII YEF

Princess Mary

'Mary, Mary, quite contrary': the nursery rhyme is thought to refer to Queen Mary I's attempts to re-impose the Catholic faith upon England, and her reputation has always been controversial. Henry's elder daughter is described as joyless and cruel, perhaps unfairly in comparison with other Tudor monarchs.

171

Henry VIII was able to swallow his disappointment that the baby Mary was not a boy. As his first surviving legitimate child, he called her his 'pearl of the world', carrying her in his arms and showing her off to courtiers.

172

Both her parents doted on her, and Mary had her own governess, and no less than four 'rockers' to rock her cradle.

173

When Mary's mother, Katherine of Aragon, fell from favour, Henry questioned the legitimacy of their marriage, and Mary's future began to look doubtful. She was demoted from 'Princess' to mere 'Lady' Mary.

174

Mary's position was further threatened by Henry's second wife Anne Boleyn. Anne hated her stepdaughter, saying 'I am her death and she is mine'. Anne found a fortune-teller willing to prophecy that she would never conceive as long and Mary and her mother remained alive.

175

Henry and Mary remained opposed on many points, including her lifelong support of her own disgraced mother. They were both very stubborn.

176

Henry pressurised Mary to renounce the Pope and recognise him as Head of the Chuch. She finally succumbed to pressure in 1526 and signed a paper stating this, and also that the marriage between him and her mother had been 'incestuous and unlawful'. (She secretly asked for Papal forgiveness for what she had done, explaining that her life had been in danger.)

177

Henry was reconciled to his elder daughter after Anne Boleyn was executed. He saw much of himself in Mary's face, and he reinstated her title of Princess. In contrast it was Mary's younger half-sister Elizabeth who was sent away after her mother's death.

178

Henry would not allow his eldest daughter to marry. 'There was nothing to be got but fine words', she said when suitors came, 'and while my father lives I shall be only the Lady Mary, the most unhappy lady in Christendom'.

179

After Henry's death, there were persistent rumours that Mary had had his tomb at Windsor opened, and his body removed and burned.

180

Henry's eldest daughter, whom he never imagined coming to the throne, reigned as Queen Mary I from 1553 until her death from cancer of the stomach on 17 November 1558.

'Mary, Mary, quite contrary, How does your garden grow? With silver bells and cockleshells, And pretty maids all in a row'

Princess Elizabeth

Red-haired like her father, clever like her mother Anne Boleyn, Henry's Elizabeth survived many obstacles to become queen. Many people think her the greatest monarch of all time.

The L. Elizabeth Prisoner in the Tower

The L. Elizabeth before her Sister Q. Mary

Queen Elizabeth rides in Triumph through Lon.

181

Elizabeth's birth in 1533 was a bitter disappointment to Henry, who was convinced Anne had been expecting a boy. His enemies were smug: 'God has forgotten him entirely, hardening him in his obstinacy to punish and ruin him' was their observation. The usual celebrations for a royal birth were perfunctory and muted, 'very cold and disagreeable'.

182

As Henry's interest in her mother waned, Elizabeth was shunned. She was kept well out of the way, and was living at a remote royal manor in Hertfordshire when Anne Boleyn was executed on 19 May 1536.

183

Henry finally came around, several wives later, when he had safely had a male heir. He brought his younger daughter back to court in 1544, showered her with attention and had her painted alongside him, Mary, Edward and Edward's mother Jane, in *The Family of Henry VIII* which hangs at Hampton Court today.

184

The King had a clever daughter. At the age of 6, Elizabeth already appeared to be grown up. Henry sent one of his under-secretaries, Thomas Wriothesley, to test her knowledge. Wriothesley observed that 'If she be no more educated that she now appeareth to me, she will prove of no less honour and womanhood than shall be seen her father's daughter'.

185

Henry's last wife, Kateryn Parr, seems to have been an affectionate stepmother. Elizabeth's first surviving letter is addressed to her, beautifully written in Italian. According to protocol, she asks her stepmother to intercede for her with her father. Kateryn saw to it that Elizabeth had good tutors.

186

Elizabeth was proud to describe herself as her father's daughter. However, there is no record that Elizabeth ever referred to or mentioned her mother, Anne Boleyn. We can only imagine what she really thought about the man who ordered the death of her mother.

187

Henry's striking red hair was inherited by Elizabeth.

188

During the reign of Elizabeth's half-sister Mary, she found herself imprisoned at the Tower under suspicion of treason. Some of the guards are supposed to have taken off their caps, knelt down, and called out 'God save your Grace' as Elizabeth passed under the Bloody Tower.

189

While Henry had running water in his bathroom at Hampton Court, Elizabeth was the first member of his family to have a flushing lavatory. It was installed for her at the palace of Richmond.

190

When Elizabeth finally became queen, she ruled for over 45 years. Her father would have been proud.

Henry's wider family

It is ironic that Henry VIII took so much trouble to try to produce heirs, but his dynasty died out in the next generation! His first son was illegitimate, although for a while this child was designated heir to Henry's throne.

191
Henry's illegitimate son, Henry Fitzroy (1519-36)

Henry was delighted with his son by Bessie Blount, an early mistress. He rewarded her well, and treated Henry handsomely too, giving him a household of his own. By 16 he was 'a most handsome, urbane and learned young gentleman', and married the Duke of Norfolk's daughter. In the absence of a legitimate son, Henry was the King's designated heir for a while. But he died just before Edward was born.

192
Henry's grandmother, Margaret Beaufort (1443-1509)

Mother of the future Henry VII, Margaret Beaufort helped lay the plans to depose Richard III, starting a chain of events which culminated in the Battle of Bosworth of 1485. 'My lady the king's mother' remained a powerful presence at court when Henry VIII was a boy. He was her favourite grandson.

193
Henry's father, Henry VII (1457-1509)

Henry VIII was very much like his father, 'with all royal gifts so representing his father than the latter seems rather to have renewed his youth than died'. Yet history has given them very different reputations: Henry VII stern, parsimonious, reserved; his son over-the-top, capricious, extravagant.

194
Henry's mother, Elizabeth of York (1466-1503)

The eldest child of King Edward IV, her marriage to Henry VII after the Battle of Bosworth signalled the reconciliation between the rival clans of York and Lancaster. She came to Hampton Court for a restful break during her last and difficult pregnancy, after which she died in 1503.

195
Henry's elder brother Arthur (1486-1502)

As a second son, Henry never expected to be king. His elder brother married Katherine of Aragon, then died of consumption at the age of 15. Henry's future as a playboy prince was over.

196
Henry's elder sister, Margaret, Queen of Scots (1489-1541)

Henry VIII's sister, Margaret, was married by proxy at the age of 13 to James IV, King of Scotland in 1503. She did her duty by becoming the mother of an heir, the future James V of Scotland.

197
Henry's younger sister, Mary, Queen of France (1496-1533)

Henry VIII was very fond of his younger sister Mary Tudor, who was thought to be 'one of the most beautiful young women in the world'. But poor Mary was married off in 1514, to Louis XII of France, gouty, toothless, and three times her age. Luckily for her he died after only a couple of months, leaving her free to marry her sweetheart Charles Brandon, Duke of Suffolk. Henry was enraged that she had dared to marry without his express permission.

198
Henry's great-niece, Lady Jane Grey (1537-54)

Henry's sister, Mary, and Charles Brandon had a son called Henry. His eldest daughter, Jane, was proposed as a rival queen to Mary when Edward VI died. Jane had a reasonably close dynastic claim and, unlike the Catholic Mary, was a strong Protestant. So her family forced her to take the throne, with the well-known consequence that she reigned for nine days before Mary I's forces deposed her, and she was executed at the Tower.

199
Henry's great niece, Mary, Queen of Scots (1542-87)

Henry's nephew James V married a Frenchwoman, and produced a daughter, Mary Stuart, later Queen of Scots. She was married to the heir to the French throne and spent much time in France. When Mary I of England died, Mary Stuart's Tudor blood made her seem a viable Catholic alternative to the Protestant Queen Elizabeth. Elizabeth I eventually had Mary, Queen of Scots, locked up, and at length she was executed at Fotheringhay Castle on 8 February 1587. However, she left behind her a son, who became both James VI of Scotland and James I of England when he inherited in 1603.

200
James VI of Scotland and I of England (1566-1625)

Elizabeth I's death in 1603 with no children meant that Henry VIII's Tudor dynasty had petered out. So the Stuarts of Scotland were invited to take her place, which is why James is the sixth king of that name in Scotland but the first in England.

From left to right: Henry Fitzroy by Lucas Horenbout, c1534; Henry VIII, Henry VII, Elizabeth of York, and Jane Seymour by Remigius van Leemput, 1667; and Mary Queen of Scots by an unknown artist, c1560-92.

16th-century gold medal (detail) depicting Henry VIII, English School.

Henry The Ruler

✤

It is tempting to regard Henry VIII as a self-willed autocrat. In reality he ruled in close conjunction with others. Being at court was being close to honour and preferment. The aristocracy, the gentry and the church all exercised influence both at the centre and in their localities. They were also all represented in parliament, providing the legislative changes and financial stability that Henry craved. The rule of law was never replaced by the rule of despotism. Henry VIII created the greatest and possibly most far-reaching legacy of his reign in the new religious organisation, forging the Church of England and Protestantism out of an international church focused on Rome and Catholicism. The royal supremacy over the church, the dissolution of the monasteries and the destruction of shrines and images, the extension of the law of treason and the start of a century of religiously-driven blood-letting all came from religious fissure worked through the rule of law.

Henry as destroyer

Monasteries provided charity, hospitality, education, employment and spiritual welfare. Henry's commissioners ruthlessly closed down over 800, destroying architectural and artistic treasures that had been at the centre of English culture for over a thousand years.

201
Swaffham Bulbeck Priory, Cambridgeshire
Destroyed 1535

The Benedictine nuns of Swaffham were poor but full of religious zeal, and they were famous as musicians. The prioress, Joan Spylman, was less than perfect, cavorting with a runaway friar and, fearing the end, sold all the corn, cattle and household goods of the monastery. After the dissolution, she suffered a breakdown and lived in an underground cave in the vicarage garden for a year.

202
Barlings Abbey, Lincolnshire
March 1537

Lincolnshire rebelled against the closure of the monasteries, and abbot Matthew Mackerel was caught up in the troubles, being accused of feeding and encouraging the rebels. This rich monastery was closed, and Mackerel and six of his brethren hanged. Our last record is of the abbot's books, unceremoniously carried away in a cart for disposal.

203
Chertsey Abbey, Surrey
18 December 1537

Chertsey was venerable, being founded in 666 by St Erkenwald. The abbot surrendered meekly, having been promised a position in a new monastery at Bisham, but that too foundered within six months through lack of food and money. Chertsey was plundered for building material for the King's palaces at Hampton Court and Oatlands.

204
Roche Abbey, Yorkshire
23 June 1538

The Cistercians of Roche worshipped an image of the crucifix found carved on a nearby rock. An eyewitness to the dissolution tells us that 'it would have made a heart of flint to have melted and wept to have seen the breaking up of the House, and their sorrowful departing'. The possessions were filched and the carved misericords and stalls burned to

melt the lead from the roof, while the tombs in the church were 'all broken, for in most abbeys were divers noble men and women, yea and in some Abbeys, kings, whose tombs were regarded no more than the tombs of all other inferior persons'.

205
St Mary de Pratis, Leicester
28 August 1538
Leicester possessed a fine library and scriptorium for copying precious manuscripts, but had fallen into debt and misbehaviour by the end of its life, when the abbot was chided for attending Mass with his fool! In 1530, the disgraced (and terminally ill) Cardinal Wolsey, *en route* to London for trial, arrived at the gates, telling the abbot 'I am come to leave my bones among you', thus cheating the King's executioner. Within a few years, his tomb was despoiled as the abbey was sacked and plundered.

206
Franciscan Friary of Coventry
5 October 1538
The old Grey Friars were famed for their biblical mystery plays, performed at the feast of Corpus Christi. King Richard III and Henry VII came to view the plays, which were performed in 92 acts, sometimes on a portable stage drawn around the streets of the town. The mayor and aldermen tried to protect the humble friars, but their pleas fell on deaf ears, and the end for both friars and their plays was swift.

207
Pipewell Abbey, Northamptonshire
5 November 1538
Unusually, Pipewell lay in a secluded glade in a forest, where Henry had hunted once in 1511. When dissolution threatened, Sir William Parre begged Cromwell to spare the abbey, but within days the monks had been turned out and their monastery was being looted by thieves; the iron and glass of the cloister windows taken while doors, locks and all other fittings from the cart-house, the salt-chamber and fish-chamber were stripped and stolen. Shortly after, a tinker was hanged at Northampton for making off with

lead and iron. Henry came back to Pipewell in 1541, but whether there was anywhere left to stay is not known.

208
Aylesford Friary, Kent
13 December 1538

Compared to enormous abbeys like Westminster, which was worth over £1000 per year, the little Carmelite friary at Aylesford yielded an income of just over £2. Just before the dissolution, two bogus commissioners arrived and tricked the friars into selling the meagre possessions of the house, thus cheating the King out of the few coppers he claimed as his own.

209
Glastonbury Abbey, Somerset
28 September 1539

The wealth of Glastonbury was legendary, with sprawling domains across many counties and one of the most important monastic libraries in Europe. The King's commissioners found the place 'great, goodly and so princely as we have not seen the like' but they were obliged to revise their reports in a more unfavourable light. Abbot Richard Whiting resisted surrender, hiding money and treasure about the buildings from the King's prying men. The commissioners swooped, finding seditious books in his

study, and through 'hard questioning' revealed 'his cankered and traitorous heart'. He was condemned, dragged to the top of Glastonbury Tor with two of his brethren, and overlooking his looted and despoiled church, hanged, drawn and quartered.

210
Waltham Abbey, Essex
23 March 1540

Waltham was the last abbey to be dissolved. It had been consecrated in 1060 in the presence of King Edward the Confessor, and the abbey claimed to have the body of King Harold, killed at the Battle of Hastings and later brought for burial by his mistress, Edith Swan-neck. With an income of £900 per year, the abbey was rich enough to pay the usual bribes to Cromwell to spare it, but all in vain. When abbot Robert Fuller handed over the keys on 23 March 1540, a thousand years of English monasticism and prayers were ended.

Henry as vandal

England's churches were crammed with holy relics, drawing pilgrims from far and wide. Overseen by Henry's chief minister, Thomas Cromwell, the relic-haters and zealous reformers of the Reformation toured the country in 1538, consigning the shrines of 'superstition and idolatry' to defacement and the fire.

211
The Holy Blood of Hailes
The greatest treasure of Hailes Abbey in Gloucestershire was the Holy Blood, a crystal phial said to contain the blood of Christ, which had been given to the abbey in 1270. When Hugh Latimer, Bishop of Worcester and relic-hater, opened the vessel, he found it contained 'an unctuous gum and a compound of many things'. It was taken to Henry VIII and then denounced by the Bishop of Rochester, who pronounced that the 'blood' was nothing more than 'honey clarified with saffron, as had been evidently proved before the king and his council'.

212
The Black Virgin of Willesden
Miraculous powers were ascribed to the ebonised statue of the Virgin at Willesden, near London. The image was pulled down in 1538, stripped of her protective garments, and with two other holy statues, Our Lady of Ipswich and Our Lady of Walsingham, burned publicly at Chelsea.

213
The tomb of Thomas Becket
Henry's wrath was especially reserved for the saintly Thomas Becket at Canterbury Cathedral, who had

From left to right:
Ruins of Hailes Abbey, once home to the Holy Blood; the tomb of Thomas Becket, 13th-century stained glass, Canterbury Cathedral; *Henry VI kneeling at the Shrine of St Edmund* in John Lydgate's *The Lives of Saints Edmund and Fremund*, 1434.

humiliated his ancestor Henry II and whose holy relics continued to attract popular adoration. The tomb-chest was described by a French pilgim as 'all covered with plates of purest gold, yet the gold is scarcely seen because it is covered with various precious stones, as sapphires, balases, diamonds, rubies and emeralds, and wherever the eye turns, something more beautiful than the rest is observed'. At its pinnacle was the 'Regale of France', an enormous ruby that had flown off the finger-ring of King Louis VII while he knelt at the shrine to pray. When the end came, the tomb was smashed up with a sledgehammer and the bones scattered and burned. It took eight strong men to lift the two giant chests containing jewels and gold, and 26 carts to remove all the other effects. The ruby was later seen adorning a ring on Henry VIII's thumb.

214

The shrine of Saint Edmund

The bones of the East Anglian king, Edmund, who died horribly at the hands of the Danes, rested in a golden feretory or tomb-chest, studded with jewels at Bury St Edmunds in Suffolk. It was the first to go, and the wreckers, though finding it 'cumbrous to deface', extracted 5,000 marks of gold and numerous jewels for the royal treasury.

215

The Rood of Grace from Boxley

The miraculous speaking image of Christ on the Cross at Boxley in Kent, when taken down and examined in 1539, was found to have wire mechanisms which moved the eyes and lips. This was a gift to the sceptics. The deception was exposed in the marketplace at Maidstone, and then again in London, where, after being denounced and ridiculed in public we are told by an eye witness that the: 'wooden trunk was hurled down neck over heels among the most crowded of the audience. And now was heard a tremendous clamour of all sorts of people; he is snatched, torn, broken in pieces bit by bit, split up into a thousand fragments, and at last thrown into the fire; and there was an end to him'. Such scenes were repeated many times, in many different locations.

216

Darvell Gadarn

By offering calves, oxen, horses or money to Darvell Gadarn, a huge wooden image of an armoured warrior in the church of Llanfihangel Llantarnam in Wales, it was believed that the pious pilgrim could be healed, saved from purgatory or even fetched out of hell. Elis Price, Cromwell's commissioner tells us that the parish priest offered him £40 to spare the image, but it was taken to London as a trophy anyway. When news reached the City that the furious parishioners were intent on marching to the capital to demand its return, the icon was taken to Smithfield, and on 22 May 1538, bound in chains in the manner of a condemned criminal, and with Thomas Forest, a priest who had denied the King's supremacy, publicly burned and its sacred power destroyed.

Pilgrim badges 14th-15th century.
Left to right: Badge of Thomas Becket with a groom holding the horse's head; pewter badge of Thomas Becket showing the mitred head of St Thomas I; lead alloy badge from Walsingham, depicting the Virgin and the Angel Gabriel; pewter pilgrim badge of Thomas Becket standing on a ship.

217
The staff of Jesus
Christ himself gave his staff to a hermit, who in turn passed it on to St Patrick. In time it became Ireland's most revered relic. It was believed that whoever swore a false oath on the staff would cause a plague. During the first stirrings of the Reformation, the archbishop stripped the relic of its golden covering and threw the staff on to the fire in Dublin's High Street.

218
The miraculous blossoms of Maiden Bradley
Richard Layton, commissioner to Thomas Cromwell visited the little priory of Maiden Bradley in Wiltshire in August 1535 to confiscate its relics, and sent by his servant 'first two flowers wrapped in white and black sarcenet that on Christmas eve, at the very hour

that Christ was born, will spring, bud and bear blossoms'. This was just a small part of the hoard, as he also sent 'a bag of relics wherein you shall see strange things, as shall appear by the scripture, as God's coat, Our Lady's smock, part of God's supper and a part of the stone on which Jesus was born in Bethlehem'.

219
Mary Magdalene's girdle
The Empress Matilda gave this precious relic to the nuns of Farleigh, near Bath, when she founded the house in the 12th century. It remained there as a much-needed source of income for almost 400 years. Women about to make a journey would come and revere the girdle, but Cromwell's man was less impressed, despatching it to London where it joined a growing collection of relics earmarked for inspection and destruction.

220
The Cross of Gneth
The altars at Henry's own chapel at Windsor were heaped up with the choicest holy relics collected by his ancestors. These included a portion of the Virgin's milk set within a crystal pot, thorns from the Crown of Thorns, bones and skulls from a myraid of holy men and women: St Bartholomew, St George, St Thomas, St Gerard, St Osyth, St Margaret, and even the jaw-bone of the Evangelist Mark (with 13 teeth). However, pride of place was given to the Cross of Gneth, a piece of the True Cross enclosed in a crystal and gold vessel, which had been a Welsh national treasure captured from Prince Llywelyn ap Gruffudd by King Edward I in 1282. This, and almost all the other relics throughout England, disappear without a trace from the record, and are never heard of again.

Ten memorable battles of Henry's reign

The most important families in Tudor Europe were the French Valois dynasty and their main rivals, the Imperial Habsburgs. Henry, galvanised by tales of English hero-kings, was eager to build an empire of his own.

The Battle of Pavia by an unknown artist, c1530.
Right: The Battle of the Spurs by an unknown artist, c1545.

221
Debacle in Gascony, 1512
This was a pitiful early attempt by Henry to make his mark in Europe, by picking a fight against the French. His Spanish allies, provided by his father-in-law Ferdinand of Aragon, failed to show up. Henry's troops either died of disease or mutinied and traipsed home.

222
Ravenna, 1512
While Henry was failing to conquer in Gascony, the French sacked Ravenna and scored a notable victory against their big rivals, the Habsburgs. Italy was the main theatre of war in the early 1500s. England was a minor player, causing trouble on Europe's margins, hoping for a share of the bigger spoils.

223
Battle of the Spurs, 1513
Henry did lead a famous cavalry charge against the French, who ran away so quickly that all that could be seen were their spurs, glinting in the sun. On canvas, Henry is shown in the centre of the action, on a white horse. Except Henry wasn't actually there. The King's Council refused to let him take part.

224
Flodden, 1513
Katherine of Aragon sat at home during Henry's early French campaigns, and amused herself by inflicting a much more horrific and brutal victory against the Scots. King James IV of Scotland was killed, and Katherine promised faithfully to send her husband his bloodstained tunic.

225
Marignano, 1515
Francis I, the new King of France, was young and ambitious and cut from the same cloth as Henry VIII. He took his own quest for European supremacy deep into Italy, capturing Milan after this bloody battle.

226
Pavia, 1525
Ten years later, however, the French

were decisively defeated by the Habsburgs at a catastrophic engagement where most of the French aristocracy were killed on the battlefield. Francis I was himself captured. He was forced to sign a humiliating treaty.

227
Sack of Rome, 1527
The Habsburgs went on to win the big game of European domination, or at least this round, in the endless and repeating cycle of continental turmoil. They captured Rome, and with it the Pope. This had terrible repercussions for Henry VIII who had hoped to persuade the Pope to grant him a divorce from his first wife.

228
Boulogne, 1544
Later in his reign, Henry decided to have a final push at emulating his medieval English heroes. He did manage to capture Boulogne from Francis I, but then faced a French counter-attack the following year in the Solent. The French raid left the ship *Mary Rose* at the bottom of the Channel. An inconclusive series of engagements led to a truce in 1546.

229
Pinkie, 1547
Henry VIII's reign is bookended with short but particularly vicious Anglo-Scottish wars. The first ended with Flodden the second, with another English victory near Musselburgh: this was the last battle fought between the royal armies of England and Scotland.

230
Wider world wars, 1509-47
There were some important military engagements taking place outside Europe while Henry VIII was on the throne. After the Battle of Panipat in 1526, Prince Babur established the Moghul Empire's 200-year rule over the Indian subcontinent. Meanwhile, across the Atlantic in 1532, a group of conquistadors led by Francisco Pizzaro defeated the Incas, and claimed the vast territory of Peru for Spain.

Ten important royal journeys

Henry VIII didn't travel much outside England.
He only went abroad four times in his whole reign, twice to wage war,
once on honeymoon, and once for a party.

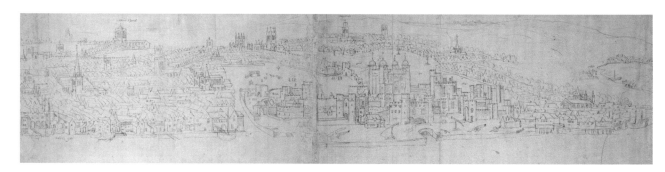

231
Henry is sent to the Tower, 1509
After the death of his father, Henry VII, in April 1509, Henry VIII left his residence in Richmond and travelled to the Tower of London. This followed the custom set by most of England's medieval monarchs before him. The Tower was the nation's oldest and most symbolic royal residence. Taking control of the Tower meant taking control of the country.

232
Henry and Katherine go to Westminster, 1509
Having made the fateful decision to marry Katherine of Aragon as soon as he became king (aged just 17), Henry took his new bride from Greenwich to Westminster Abbey to be crowned in a joint ceremony on 24 June. They then crossed the road for a banquet in Westminster Hall, 'greater than any Caesar had known'.

233
Henry's pilgrimage to Walsingham, 1511
Two years into the reign, Katherine gave birth to a little prince. Henry was overjoyed and rode out to Norfolk on a pilgrimage of thanksgiving at the shrine of Our Lady of Walsingham. Henry's son lived less than two months, and Katherine would never provide Henry with another living son.

234
Henry goes to France in 1513
Anxious beyond measure to prove that he was a true Renaissance Prince and bonafide English hero, Henry VIII took personal command of his armies and set off for France to meet his new ally, the Habsburg Holy Roman Emperor, Maximilian I. The campaign lasted just four months, but brought Henry a notable victory and the capture of Tournai, the fourth largest French city. More importantly still, this brought him some measure of European recognition and a seat at the negotiating table.

235
Henry goes to France in 1520
The next time Henry crossed the Channel, with his entire court, was for the three-week jamboree known as the Field of Cloth of Gold. This was ostensibly a political summit with the new French King, Francis I, but it was also an enormously expensive party, Henry blew about one-seventh of his entire annual income on the desperate extravagance of the transport arrangements, the gold tents, the food – and the wine!

236
Henry and Anne Boleyn go to Boulogne, 1532

In the next round of European summits, Henry travelled to Boulogne, once again to meet Francis I. Significantly, he took with him Anne Boleyn, even though he had yet to fully extricate himself from his first marriage. It was probably during this rather premature honeymoon that Henry finally persuaded Anne into bed.

237
Henry goes to Rochester to meet Anne of Cleves, 1540

On New Year's Day, Henry arrived at Rochester Abbey in disguise to surprise his new bride. He found her in a chamber looking out of the window, and 'suddenly embraced and kissed her… and she being abashed and not knowing who it was thanked him, but regarded him little'. The marriage never really got over this unpromising start.

238
Royal Progress to York, 1541

In the summer of 1541, Henry VIII took Catherine Howard on an extensive tour of the north, ostensibly to inspect his northern defences and to visit his local administrators, but also to show off his fifth wife, 30 years his junior.

239
Henry goes to France in 1544

Despite being by now enormous, and unwell, Henry embarked on a last military fling towards the end of his reign. He did capture Boulogne in September, but was immediately left in the lurch (again) by his Imperial allies; Henry did not have the money or the energy to follow up this success, and France eventually bought back Boulogne in 1550.

240
Henry's last journey, 1547

Henry died in the early hours of 28 January 1547 at Whitehall Palace. His monstrously bloated corpse was then conveyed in a solemn, and lengthy funeral procession to Windsor. Henry was buried with Jane Seymour.

Previous page: The Embarkation of Henry VIII at Dover, by an unknown artist, c1545. Left: A 16th-century view of the Tower of London by Anthonis van den Wyngaerde. Below: The Field of Cloth of Gold by an unknown artist, c1545.

Ten acts of Parliament

Henry VIII usually had a specific reason for calling Parliament, the most common being to grant money. However, during the 'Reformation Parliament' of 1529-36, some of the most momentous legislation of any age was passed.

241
Subsidy, 1512
In order to wage war against France, Henry VIII needed to raise taxation, which he could only do through parliament. The King was awarded taxes known as 'a fifteenth and tenth', and also what was euphemistically known as a 'subsidy'. The taxes were progressive, in that dukes paid £6 13s 4d (£6.66), labourers paid 6d (2.5p), servants and apprentices 4d (2p).

242
Act of Appeals, 1533
The first shot in the war of words with Rome leading to the break of the Reformation, this act ensured that appeals from English courts 'in such cases as have been used to be pursued to the see of Rome shall not be from henceforth had nor used but within this realm'. By creating a self-contained system and effectively a national church rather than deferring to an international church, Henry VIII was setting down the road to rupture.

243
Buggery Act, 1533
Those found guilty of the 'detestable and abominable Vice of Buggery committed with mankind or beast' could be put to death, and all their goods and chattels confiscated.

The act, to be reissued many times, took punishment for homosexuality away from the church and into the main common law courts. In reality it was a piece of tidying-up legislation that met a pressing and present need. Yet the death penalty remained on the statute book until 1861 (and the last execution under the law happened in 1836).

244
Act of Supremacy, 1534
A further step in the break with Rome came through the passage of this act making 'the King's Highness to be Supreme Head of the Church of England and to have authority to reform and redress all errors, heresies and abuses in the same'. Secular political authority replaced ecclesiastical power in creating the Church of England. Failure to accept this new state of affairs brought such eminent men as Thomas More and John Fisher to the scaffold.

245
Act of the Governance of Wales, 1534
This act was effectively a means to annexe Wales properly to England and to bring greater order. As the preamble stated, 'the people of Wales and marches of the same, not dreading the good and wholesome laws and statutes of this realm, have of long time continued and persevered in perpetration and commission of divers and manifold thefts, murders, rebellions, wilful burning of houses and other scelerous deeds and abominable malefact', and so it was time that they stopped.

246
Treasons Act, 1534
By bringing the existing law of 1352 up to date and providing legal safeguards for his new position in the Church, the act 'whereby divers offences be made high treason' was the strongest weapon in Henry VIII's armoury of judicial terror. Passed in the immediate aftermath of the Act of Supremacy, this gave the regime the right to move against 'all cankered and traitorous hearts, willers and workers of the same', that is, all those who did not agree with the new laws.

247
Dissolution of the Monasteries, 1536
Although the monasteries were not an initial or necessary target in the Reformation process, they were an easy target. Stories of fat abbots, concubines, loose living and fleecing credulous pilgrims circulated widely. Under Thomas Cromwell, the first wave dissolving 'all religious houses of monks, canons and nuns' with a value below £200 and where 'manifest sin,

vicious, carnal and abominable living
is daily used and committed' began in
1536. The secularisation of land had
been demanded by many for a long
time, and now the chance was there.

248
Act extinguishing the authority of the Bishop of Rome, 1536

This was the final element in the
establishment of the royal supremacy
over the Church and subsequently the
vesting of the royal authority in Thomas
Cromwell as spiritual vice-gerent.

249
Act of Proclamations, 1539

'An act that proclamations made by the
King shall be obeyed' was designed to
contradict those 'divers and numerous
froward [sic], wilful and obstinate
persons' who declared that only laws
enacted in parliament were valid. The
royal prerogative, jealously guarded by
Tudor and Stuart monarchs, was not to
be undermined.

250
Parish registers order, 1537

One of the longest-lasting of all the
reforms of Henry VIII's reign, Thomas
Cromwell's order for each parish to
maintain registers of baptisms, marriages
and funerals resulted in a system that has
survived in essence to the present day.

Henry VIII's Knights of the Garter from the *Black Book of the Garter* (detail), 1534.

Henry's Court

❀

The magnificence and ostentation of palace life are among the great and lasting memories of Henry VIII's era. The royal court, where political society and authority assembled, was a nation in microcosm. Strict rules of organisation and precedence governed it. The outside departments were under the control of the Master of the Horse. Indoors it was divided into two. The Household, with all the services and support required for hundreds of people, came under the Lord Steward. The Chamber, beyond the Great Hall and overseen by the Lord Chamberlain, was where important people were to be found and where important business was conducted. Political power was concentrated among the men who attended to the King's needs in the magnificent but close confines of the inner Privy Chamber. Intrigue was everywhere. Everything was concentrated upon the King, everybody danced attendance upon him, and when he emerged from the innermost areas to process to the Chapel Royal, all eyes and ears were upon him.

The best and worst jobs of the Tudor court

The hundreds employed at court must have been the envy of the general Tudor population, although life wasn't all roses for the scullions and gong-scourers!

Best Jobs

251
Lord Chamberlain
A powerful position, with responsibility for court ceremony, and for all the people who worked in the royal rooms: chaplains, physicians, waiters at the royal table, musicians and guards.

253
Master of the Tents and Revels
This must have been a fun job, with responsibility for staging masques, parties and entertainments. A career highlight must have been the great tournament, The Field of Cloth of Gold *(below)* where a vast array of splendid temporary accomodation was needed.

255
Groom of the Stool
This was a very important and prominent position as the Groom, head of the Gentlemen of the Bedchamber, was physically closest to the King. However, there was a drawback that might also qualify this job as one of the worst. You had to wipe the King's bottom!

252
Lord Steward
The head of the other great department of the Royal Household, in charge of about 500 men (and a handful of women) responsible for all the 'below stairs' services.

254
Pudding-maker
There were only five or six women in the Royal Household, including the laundresses, and Mrs Cornwallis, who 'makes the King's puddings'. She was rewarded with a house in London.

Worst jobs

256
Weeder
Some of the few women around the court did back breaking work as 'weeders in the King's garden'.

257
Gong-scourer
The palace garderobes (lavatories) discharged into brick latrines, known euphemistically in the 16th century as 'gongs'. These needed regular cleaning by an unfortunate group of servants who had to climb into the pits and scrub out the accumulated filth, by candlelight!

258
Scullion
'Once in the forenoone and one in the afternoone', it was the scullions' job to 'sweepe and cleane the courts, outward galleryes, and other places of the court, soe as there remaine no filth or uncleannesse in the same'.

259
Cook
It was hot and dirty in the kitchens, sometimes unbearably so. Often the boys turning the spits found themselves 'interlarding their own grease to help the drippings'.

260
Any lower servant
There were those who has to sleep in one of the common areas, like the Great Hall. Alexander Barclay, a visitor to court, described a terrible night spent with the other servants:

'Some buck and some babble, some cometh drunk to bed, Some brawl and some jangle, when they be beastly fed, Some laugh and some cry, each man will have his will, Some spew and some piss, not one of them is still.'

Left to right: Charles Brandon, Duke of Suffolk, Henry's Lord Steward; *The Field of Cloth of Gold* (detail); a cook gutting a hare; 16th-century bakers.

Ten royal craftsmen and gardeners

Henry's palaces were created by an army of craftsmen and gardeners, some drawn from among the finest in Europe. Their efforts dazzled visitors to the King's residences.

261
Galyon Hone, glazier
Glass was the most conspicuous way of showing wealth and power, and Henry commissioned acres of it from his Dutch glazier, Galyon Hone. Documents record him again and again at the King's various houses, making windows and filling them with coloured badges and heraldic devices for the queen's closet and bedchamber.

262
James Nedeham, engineer
A great carpenter and engineer, Nedeham's abilities had been recognised by Cardinal Wolsey, and Henry was no fool, taking him into service and promoting him to the position of Surveyor of the King's Works, overseeing all the royal building projects. The magnificent Great Hall ceiling at Hampton Court is one of his finest achievements.

263
Roger Lock, carpenter
At Canterbury, a team of 89 carpenters worked day and night to build 'the great vault' over the roof of the new palace there, sawing the timbers into 'posts, reason pieces, interstices, beams, purlins, principals, rafters, puncheons, pole plates, joists, summers, wind-beams, mountains, gounsells and other pieces requisite and ready'.

264
John Hethe, painter
Henry's palaces were often adorned with colour splashed over every available surface, particularly floors and ceilings that could look incredibly flamboyant. One prominent painter was John Hethe of London, whom we know gilded weather vanes about the palaces, and painted arms and badges at Hampton Court.

265
Stephen Parrett, brickmaker
The King needed bricks in enormous quantities for his endless building projects, and Stephen Parrett of Deptford was one brickmaker who provided two million of them for the King's project at Dartford in summer 1541.

266
Alice Rokke, gardener

Even the humblest servants warrant a mention in the records. Alice Rokke was a weeder in the King's privy garden, paid threepence for a day's backbreaking work – half the rate for a man.

267
Henry Blankston, carver
The wonders of Henry's interiors would have been poorer without the services of Henry Blankston, a carver

of English or German origin. He garnished the galleries at Hampton Court 'with a border of busy antique with the mermaids antique all gilded'.

268

Nicholas Bellin, designer

Nicholas Bellin of Modena had been a trusted 'valet de garderobe' to the French King Francis I, working at Fontainebleau. When he was involved in a plot to defraud the King, he fled to England, from where Francis strenuously tried to have him extradited. Never one to miss a chance to get one up on his rival Francis, Henry instead employed Bellin, and he designed Henry's tomb.

269

Nicholas Oursian, horologer

Henry loved clocks, and had a whole room devoted to them. His French horologer, or clock maker, enjoyed a salary of fourpence per day to maintain the collection. Oursian's great astronomical device still graces Anne Boleyn's Gateway at Hampton Court.

270

John of Padua, artificer

The Tudors would not understand the term 'architect' as we know it; the nearest they got was a 'deviser of buildings'. John of Padua, an Italian is described as such when Henry gave him a pension for his skill as an artificer, engineer and musician.

Left to right: The arms of Henry VIII and Jane Seymour, stained glass, *c*1536; the Pond Gardens at Hampton Court; a late 15th-century gardener; carved wooden 'eavesdroppers' from the ceiling of the Great Hall; the Astronomical Clock.

Eating at court

While an average Tudor family would have lived on a diet of stewed vegetables and pulses, a Tudor courtier enjoyed a wide variety of food. The King himself was offered a tempting array of at least 13 freshly-cooked dishes at every meal.

Food for the King

271

Henry usually ate in his private rooms. On more formal occasions he took his seat alone at a high covered table in the Presence Chamber, under the canopy of state.

272

The King's food was prepared by Henry's own French chef in a private kitchen below his rooms. This ensured that the food could be brought hot to his table whenever he was ready to eat.

273

A servant known as the 'sewer' would wash Henry's hands in heated and scented water, and dry them on a linen towel. Then, on bended knee, Gentlemen and Ushers of his Privy Chamber would serve the King.

274

Every day the King would choose from a huge buffet, sampling whatever took his fancy. Dishes included a variety of game, in pies and roasted, heron and swan, conger eel and even porpoise, a new and exotic treat. Sweet dishes were often served with savoury; Henry would have been tempted by delicious custards, fritters and jellies, and cream of almond.

Henry VIII dining in his Presence Chamber; *Right*: The Tudor Kitchens at Hampton Court.

275

The King drank choice wines, first tasted by his cupbearer, from Venetian glass or alabaster cups.

Food for the court

276

Depending on their rank, the rest of the court ate in the Great Watching Chamber, the Great Hall, the kitchens, or wherever they could or were permitted to eat according to the rules as drawn up by the Lord Chamberlain.

277

A courtier was entitled to two meals a day, served at 10am and 4pm. In 1526 there were 600 courtiers entitled to eat in the Great Hall at Hampton Court. They were served in two sittings.

278

Each meal had two courses, served in 'messes' – dishes that would be shared between four people.

279

Higher ranking courtiers ate in the Great Watching Chamber where the food was better and the choice greater. The superior dishes, as they were carried through the Great Hall, were the envy of the lower status diners eating at their long tables.

280

At court it was considered rude to finish everything on the table; the lower orders depended on leftovers, known as 'manners'. These were collected in a voider or great basket for distribution to the poor at the palace gate.

'Table manners,' as we understand today, were also very important, and the Dutch writer Erasmus published *De Civitate* in 1534. A couple of his suggestions:
Sit not down until you have washed. Don't shift your buttocks left and right as if to let off some blast. Sit neatly and still. A gobbit that can't be taken easily with the hand, take it on your trencher.

**Dynner
First course**

*Cheat bread and manchett
Ale and beare
Wyne
Herring
Pottage [a thick broth]
Orgaine Lyng [cod]
Poudred Eales or Lampons
Pyke
Calver Salmon
Whyting
Haddocks, Mullets or Basses
Playce or Gunard
Sea Breame or Soalles
Congers, Door
Purpose [porpoise], seal
Carpe, Trout
Crabbes, Lobsters
Custard
Rascalles or Flage
[cuts of venison]
Tarte closed
Frytter
Fruit*

**Dynner
Second course**

*Second pottage
Stergeion
Tench [carp]
Perch or other dish
Eles with lampreys roast
Chynes of salmon broiled
Crevez [crayfish]
Shrympes
Tarte
Fritter
Fruit
Baked pepins [apples], oranges
Butter and eggs*

Ten lost palaces

Henry was the greatest builder of his age, often acquiring modest houses and enlarging them on a massive scale. Despite lavish expenditure, few outlasted the King, and of those that remained after his death, almost all have disappeared.

281

Ampthill in Bedfordshire was primarily used for hunting, though it served a second, more useful purpose when Henry used its relative isolation to shut away Katherine of Aragon while divorce proceedings dragged on.

282

Grafton in Northamptonshire was a great hunting destination; 'a fair manor with goodly parks and lands about'. When Henry trudged northwards to York in the summer of 1541, torrential rain forced him to stay there for an unprecedented two weeks.

283

Henry was born at Greenwich Palace, and spent much time there. Sports and pastimes are often mentioned, with tennis, archery and even hand-gun practice being favoured pursuits.

Animals were also abundant. The court enjoyed bear-baiting and cock-fighting, kennels were kept for the hounds, and even a hawk mews provided the King with yet more sport. In 1534, timber coops were made 'for the peycocke and the peylycune that were brought to the king out of the new found land'. That Christmas holes were dug in the courtyard and tree branches set into the ground 'for the lord of misrule and his company to hunt the wild boar with his hounds to show the King and the queen pastime'.

284

Nonsuch in Surrey dazzled visitors with its mixture of timber-framing, brick and stucco, painted, gilded and decorated over almost every surface. When it was completed in 1541 it had 60-foot high octagonal towers. The diarist John Evelyn has left us a vivid description

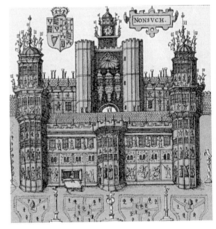

of the two courts, castle-like, with the walls 'incomparably beautified'. He saw many of the wall surfaces covered with hanging slates, some shaped like fish scales, and carvings everywhere. Nonsuch lasted until the late 17th century, before being sold for salvage. Archaeologists have revealed fragments of its once great riches.

Left to right: Greenwich Palace, Nonsuch Palace and a 16th-century map of England showing the location of Henry's lost palaces.

285

A simple lawn within the castle walls at Hertford is all that remains of a great Tudor lodging. Henry stopped visiting when he found that he suffered from the 'sweating sickness' while there, but the King's children were often sent to Hertford for long periods. By 1566 the building was in great decay 'and will if speedy remedy be not provided fall into utter ruin'. Ruinous it became, so that nothing is visible today except a fine gatehouse.

286

Henry took a fancy to a city merchant's house at Oatlands in Surrey, and swapped it for another property. The dissolved buildings of Chertsey Abbey (see page 64) provided ample building materials, and its forests were denuded for the new palace's roofs. By the time it was completed

it had everything requisite for the King, including a polygonal tower, with a ceiling decorated with painted clouds. Oatlands long outlasted Henry, but disappeared during the Commonwealth.

287

Richmond had one of the longest and

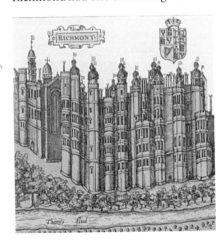

most distinguished pedigrees as a royal palace, being favoured by medieval kings. Henry VII had constructed great lodgings after a disastrous fire in 1497, but his son was less enthusiastic, and gave the palace to Wolsey. The Cardinal improved it at great cost, only to lose it, and later the King bestowed it on Anne of Cleves. The palace was demolished during the Commonwealth, and only the gatehouse remains.

288

Whitehall had, like Hampton Court, been confiscated from Cardinal Wolsey. There, Henry 'most sumptuously builded and edified many... beautiful, costly and pleasant lodgings, buildings and mansions for his grace's singular pleasure, comfort and commodity, to the great honour of his highness and of this realm'. Today, Whitehall is the

centre of government, but just one tiny fragment of Henry's palace survives, next to No. 10 Downing Street.

289

Henry rarely ventured outside the south-east, but when he did so, preparations had to be made. On his great journey to the north in 1541, the former St Mary's Abbey in York was converted to the 'King's Manor'. Even as the court moved north that summer, the French ambassador noted how 1,500 men swarmed over the buildings in a frantic effort to make the palace ready. Much effort and money was expended for a single visit: Henry never ventured north again.

290

Pontefract Castle must have appeared as a fairy-tale castle with its many towers and turrets. For Henry it provided only bad memories. During a stay there in 1541, under his very nose, his queen Catherine Howard had carried out her adulterous liaisons with Thomas Culpeper.

Five winners...

Henry could spot talent, and bright men could prosper at his court, particularly those with charm and wit to match the King's own.

> 'You often boast to me that you have the king's ear and have fun with him, freely... This is like having fun with tamed lions – often it is harmless... but just as often there is fear of harm. Often he roars in rage for no known reason, and suddenly the fun becomes fatal.'
>
> Sir Thomas More

Left to right: Sir Thomas Wyatt by Hans Holbein the Younger, c1535; Thomas Cranmer, by Gerlach Flicke 1545; Richard Rich by Holbein, 1536 and Stephen Gardiner, English School, 16th century.

Winners

291
The Rival – Sir Thomas Wyatt (1503-42)

Poet and courtier. Although one of Henry's trusted diplomats, it's possible that Wyatt was in love with Anne Boleyn in the early 1520s, and in May 1536 he was one of those arrested and sent to the Tower on suspicion of being one of her lovers. He narrowly escaped Anne's fate and that of the five men who died with her, and was released on 14 June. He wrote, 'these bloody days have broken my heart', but he recovered sufficiently to succeed in positions of authority at court and abroad.

292
The Fixer – Thomas Cranmer (1489-1556)

Archbishop of Canterbury. Henry rewarded this academic cleric, who had found legal and historical precedents to support the break with Rome, by making him Archbishop in 1533. Cranmer helped shape the English Reformation. He had the unenviable task of telling Henry of Catherine Howard's infidelities, but his simplicity, humility and wisdom kept the King's favour, despite several plots against him by his enemies in the 1540s.

293
The social climber – Thomas Cawarden (*c*1514-59)

Courtier. Son of a London clothworker, he attracted the attention of Cromwell and rose to become close to the King as a Gentleman of the Privy Chamber by 1540, and Master of the Revels from 1544. His star continued to rise: Henry was so fond of Cawarden that he left his favoured courtier £200 'in token of special love' in his will. Cawarden continued to serve under Edward, Mary and Elizabeth, and died a very wealthy man.

294
The ruthless chancer – Richard Rich (*c*1496-1567)

Rich, who rose from the Middle Temple to become Solicitor-General in 1533, could be relied on to do Henry's dirty work. He specialised in interrogating political prisoners: it was on his word that Sir Thomas More and Bishop John Fisher went to their deaths, and he allegedly racked the heretic Anne Askew with his own hands. Rich was executor of Henry's will and went on to become a baron under Edward VI and Lord Chancellor of England.

295
The diplomat – Stephen Gardiner, Bishop of Winchester (*c*1495-1555)

A protégé of Cardinal Wolsey, Gardiner's legal and diplomatic skills soon brought him to Henry's attention. He became the King's principal secretary, working to secure his divorce from Katherine of Aragon. He was rewarded with the wealthy and important bishopric of Winchester, but his career took a downturn in the 1530s, when he was suspected of opposing Henry's religious policies. The fall of Thomas Cromwell (in which Gardiner probably had a hand) paved the way for his return to favour, and he remained one of the leading figures at court, where he played a key role in foreign affairs and continued to resist radical religious change.

And five losers

*But while rewards were high, so were the risks.
Those who failed to please could fall with terrifying speed.*

296

The foolish young noble – Henry Howard, Earl of Surrey (1517-47)

Poet, nobleman and courtier. The son of Thomas Howard, the third Duke of Norfolk, Surrey was one of the most powerful noblemen in the country and of regal descent. He became a close friend to the King's illegitimate son, Henry Fitzroy, Duke of Richmond with whom he was brought up at Windsor. He married Lady Frances de Vere, came to court in 1536 and served the King in a variety of capacities, especially in the 1540s war against France. He was, however, also prone to bouts of riotous behaviour, and twice imprisoned. In 1546, he flaunted his Plantagenet ancestry, boldly quartering the royal arms into his own heraldic bearings, which looked like a claim to the throne. Surrey was tried for treason and beheaded on 19 January 1547, nine days before Henry's death.

297

The wily politician – Thomas Cromwell, Earl of Essex (1485-1540)

The son of a south London brewer-blacksmith, the clever and dynamic Cromwell so impressed Henry VIII that he made him the second most powerful man in England. Cromwell had first made his mark as legal adviser to Cardinal Wolsey, and was appointed as Henry's first minister in 1533. Henry knighted him three years later, which brought Cromwell a host of fancy titles: Lord Privy Seal, Baron Cromwell, and Vice-gerent in Spirituals, effectively exercising the newly established royal supremacy on Henry's behalf. From this position of power, he suddenly toppled – and in July 1540 was executed, shortly after having been created Earl of Essex. His fall is something of a mystery. Possible reasons are the failed marriage to Anne of Cleves, pushing the King towards a more evangelical line in religion, overreaching himself, or the work of his enemies like Norfolk and Gardiner, but none seem to explain it sufficiently.

298

The childhood friend – Sir Nicholas Carew (1496-1538)

Carew was Henry VIII's childhood friend, sporting companion and favourite courtier, but ended up hanged, drawn and quartered as a traitor on the King's orders. At his height, in 1522, he was made Master of the Horse, a prestigious and influential post at court, and he was very wealthy, with lands worth £400 (the third highest figure among the King's household servants). Although Carew sympathised with Katherine of Aragon, he seems to have retained Henry's friendship until 1538, when he responded angrily to an insult from

the King, and fell swiftly from favour at court. Cromwell presented Henry with evidence of Carew's involvement in the traitorous Exeter conspiracy (see below), and his fate was sealed.

299

The martyr – Sir Thomas More (1478-1535)

Lord Chancellor, scholar and humanist. With a background as a classical scholar and lawyer, More joined the King's council in 1517-18, and was knighted in 1521. He served on overseas delegations, and became secretary to Cardinal Wolsey, before succeeding Wolsey to become Henry VIII's first minister in 1529, and Lord Chancellor. Henry valued and admired the learning and wisdom of the elder man, but More's principles were to be his undoing. Although he ignored More's snub to Anne Boleyn (More did not attend her coronation) Henry could not overlook his refusal to swear an oath to the 1534 Act of Succession, which rejected papal supremacy. More was tried in 1535 for denying the King's title of Supreme Head of the Church of England and found guilty. Although sentenced to a traitor's death, Henry had this commuted to beheading, and More died on 6 July 1535.

300

The favourite cousin – Henry Courtenay, Marquess of Exeter (c1498-1538)

For Courtenay, being Henry's cousin was both a blessing and a curse. For nearly 30 years, Exeter was a member of Henry VIII's inner circle, but the simmering tensions between the Marquess and Thomas Cromwell erupted in 1536, when the latter accused Courtenay of favouring Princess Mary as the King's successor. Although he had been restored to royal favour by October 1537, when his wife carried the infant Prince Edward at his christening, Exeter's days were numbered. A year later, he was one of a group of men arrested for allegedly desiring the King's death and plotting to restore England to the Catholic church. By Christmas 1538, the King's long-term favourite had been executed as a traitor.

Left to right: Henry Howard, Earl of Surrey, attributed to William Scrots, 1546; Thomas Cromwell, Earl of Essex, after Hans Holbein the Younger, 1533-4; Nicholas Carew by Holbein, 1532-3; Thomas More at the Tower with his daughter by William Frederick Yeames, 1863.

The Great Hall at
Hampton Court, and
(right) its stained glass
window (19th century),
showing Henry and the
badges of all his wives
and children.

Ten types of palatial room

Henry's palaces were defined by the magnificent rooms that were the settings for processions and for court ceremonies, and that made suitable venues for the presence of the mighty sovereign himself.

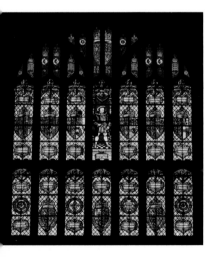

301
Great Hall

The great hall was the centre of court life: a great room for public functions and where the grandest architecture could be displayed. Richmond was a particularly fine example, 'not beamed nor braced but proper knots correctly carved, joined and set together with mortices and pinned, hanging pendant from the said roof into the ground and floor, and after the most new invention and craft of the pure practice of geometry'.

302
Gallery

The gallery was a new room in the 16th century, part covered walkway for exercise, part art gallery, but most palaces had one. Henry liked Wolsey's gallery at Esher so much, he had it dismantled and re-erected at Whitehall, where it was filled with maps in gilded frames.

303
Study

At Eltham in c1518, Thomas Forster records making a floor over the King's pew on the south side of his closet in order to form a study, furnished with 'coffers', 'almoryes' and desks with locks and keys.

304
King's closet

The closet was a small withdrawing room, forming a private space or a buffer between rooms. At Richmond the privy closet was 'richly hanged with silk and travasse carpet and cushions'.

305
Privy Chamber

This fine room displaying the best craftsmanship was part of the State Apartments established by Henry. At Greenwich in 1533 the fret ceiling was embellished with 67 bullions (gold blocks) and 218 buds by Andrew Wright and John Hethe. Later they came back to paint out the pomegranate badges of Katherine of Aragon.

306
Queen's bedchamber
In Anne Boleyn's chamber at Greenwich Palace, a false roof was constructed to hang a cloth of arras for privacy while the Queen was in labour, as well as a 'cupboard of state' to display her plate, and a 'great bed of estate'. Two folding tables were made, one as a breakfast table, and the other 'for her grace to play upon'.

307
Paradise Chamber
Several palaces have records of an enigmatic room called a 'Paradise Chamber'. One of these glittered with gold, silver and jewels, and planets displayed in an astronomical scheme.

308
Chapel
Henry's chapels were magnificent and extravagant. The ceiling of the Chapel Royal at Hampton Court is breathtaking. The chapel at Richmond was 'well paved, glazed, and hung with cloth of arras, the body and the quire with cloth of gold and the altars set with many relics, jewels and full rich plate'.

309
Bathroom
Though he may not have bathed frequently, Henry had his own bathroom, with the bath heated by a fire, so that the King could soak and poach slowly. Other mortals had to wash themselves with cold water drawn from cisterns in the courtyards. Contamination was a concern. At Greenwich Palace these were painted with crosses so that 'none should piss against them'.

310
Lodgings
Many rooms in the palace are referred to in the records simply as lodgings. This could mean anything from a simple room for a minor courtier, containing little more than a bed and a piss-pot, to a magnificent suite fit for a visiting sovereign.

The King's furniture

Large, extravagant buildings needed impressive, exaggerated pieces of furniture and decoration. Henry commissioned extra-ordinary objects to fill his grand chambers and his private, more intimate spaces.

Oak-carved bedhead decorated with the monogram of Henry VIII and Anne of Cleves.

311

Whether Henry was there or not, the Chair of State was the seat of authority and warranted a bow in its own right. A 16th-century set of rules notes gravely that 'no manner of what so ever degree he be' no one could 'come nigh the king's chair nor stand under the cloth of estate'.

312

The King's bed was wainscoted and gilded. One bill shows that six carvers worked on a walnut bed for ten months, after which it was gilded. When it was made every morning and the embroidered curtains drawn, the bed was sprinkled and blessed with holy water.

313

While lesser mortals used the communal 'jakes' or lavatories, Henry had his own comfortable 'close stool' or stool chamber. An account survives for Harmond West to make six close stools for various palaces, firstly wainscoted and dressed with calf and sheepskins, black velvet and silk, ribbons, a fringe, gilt nails and soft scarlet kersey (a woollen cloth), all embroidered and provided with a burnished pewter pan in its own leather carrying box.

314

Henry's longing for a son often manifested itself in wishful thinking. Mindful of the many lost children of Katherine of Aragon, Henry took no chances when Anne Boleyn was pregnant in 1536, and ordered lodgings to be refurbished 'for the coming of the prince'. These included a decorated cradle with an iron canopy and other objects for the royal birth. She miscarried – a son – at three months.

315

Cabinets or 'almoryes' appear in the records, and were needed to keep precious objects safe. We learn that Henry had these to store tennis rackets, clocks and needlework samples.

316

Great trussing coffers are mentioned in many inventories. These were constructed of solid oak, and 'trussed' with iron bands, with complex locks for the safe keeping of the King's plate and other treasures.

317

As Henry grew more corpulent and suffered from gout, special chairs called 'trammes' were made 'for the king's majesty to sit in to be carried to and fro in his galleries and chambers'.

318

Tables were to be found in many rooms, often robust pieces at which the council of state might meet or communal dining occur. In the private chambers, more delicate pieces sufficed. The queen, for example had a table 'with folding leaves for her grace to break her fast upon'.

319

During the summer, when the fires were not lit, screens covered the fireplace, either as painted or tapestry panels, or perhaps as a piece of panelling, 'with the King's arms and feet of lions, dragons and greyhounds'.

320

Did Henry's windows have curtains? Almost certainly. At Eltham Palace the bay windows in his lodgings were provided with iron rods with rings and hooks 'for to hang tappetts' – most probably tapestry curtains.

Swearing in Tudor

Anyone at the Tudor court who used 'proud and opprobrious words' could expect to be challenged to a duel, unless they were the King, of course. What sorts of insults did Henry and others fling around at the court?

Ambassadors from the King of France before Henry VIII at Hampton Court, by William Kent (1685?-1748).

321

When Henry was in a bad mood, he used to call his minister Thomas Wriothesley 'my pig'.

322

When in an even worse mood, he called this (usually) favoured official: 'Knave! Arrant knave! Beast! And fool!'

323

According to Henry, the French were 'cruel, impious, criminal and unspeakable'.

324

Lots of people hated Anne Boleyn, so she came in for some very inventive insults. Some people called her the 'goggle-eyed whore'.

325

Anne Boleyn got her own back when her fool castigated the crowds reluctant to cheer the unpopular new queen at her coronation procession. 'I think you have scurvy heads, and dare not uncover!' she called out to spectators who had failed to doff their hats.

326

Fools or minstrels were popular members of the Tudor court. They provided 'harping and carping', music and jokes, and sometimes dancing and acrobatics. 'Sir, what say ye with your fat face?' was a common jibe to an indulgent audience of courtiers.

327

The King's temper got worse as he got older. In his later years, one courtier remembered Henry VIII as a terrifying tyrant, raging and swearing that 'there was not a head so fine as he would not make it fly'.

328

In his book against Luther, *The Defence of the Seven Sacraments*, Henry VIII has a go at Luther. He calls him 'a venomous serpent', (and) 'infernal wolf' (and a) 'detestable trumpeter of pride, calumnies and schism'.

329

In return, Luther called Henry VIII a 'deaf adder, (a) miserable scribbler (and a) fool!'

330

Once Anne Boleyn and Henry were married, her enemies hated the new badges that began to appear all over the royal palaces showing hers and the King's initials entwined 'HA'. Disapproving courtiers said that the new queen was a joke, and that the symbol (really Henry and Anne) stood for Ha! Ha! Ha!

IMPERATOR MAXIMILIAN

HERIGVS OCTAVVS REX ANGLIÆ

The Meeting of Henry VIII and the Emperor Maximilian I (detail) by an unknown artist, c1545.

HENRY'S WORLD

❀

Around Henry VIII, a new European order was emerging. The power of France was increasingly hemmed in by the merged dynasties that ruled Spain, the Netherlands and the Holy Roman Empire (encompassing modern Germany and beyond). The power of Islam in the Ottoman Empire to the east was an ominous and growing threat. Henry VIII struck an increasingly important figure in this milieu. It was an age when the printing press came into its own, as ideas and words swept across Europe, and when the tendrils of Renaissance art, architecture and thought began to penetrate England. After long periods of economic and population stagnation, towns, industries and numbers began to grow, at home and abroad. The England and Europe of 1547 were both quite different places from the England and Europe of 1509.

Ten famous books of Henry's reign

For the educated, it was an exciting time to be a reader in England as the development of print technology accelerated the spread of ideas.

331
The Coverdale Bible

This was the first complete printed translation of the Bible into English. Miles Coverdale launched his book into the midst of the English Reformation in 1535 from the relative safety of Antwerp. Henry VIII moved quickly to ensure that any such Bible was an officially sanctioned one, so Coverdale was invited to England instead to oversee production of the Great Bible (see below).

332
The Great Bible

The first official English printed Bible of 1539. The title page has a big picture of Henry, lording it over his temporal and spiritual realm as the newly, self-crowned, Supreme Head of the new Church of England. Kings and bishops kneel before Henry the Emperor holding an imperial sword in one hand and delivering the new English Bible with the other.

333
The *Valor Ecclesiasticus*

Not so much a book, but a multi-volume list. When Henry VIII broke with the Church of Rome in 1534, he commissioned this comprehensive survey of ecclesiastical wealth, so that he could tax it, and ultimately seize it or sell it.

334
The *Bishop's Book* and the *King's Book*

As Henry and his ecclesiastical apologists tried to sort out the theological framework for the break with Rome, various tracts and proclamations were issued. The *Bishop's Book* of 1537 moved the new Anglican Church toward a reformed Protestant position, but the *King's Book* of 1543 reflected Henry's own uncomfortable retention of much Catholic doctrine.

TOPIENSIVM ALPHABETVM.
e f g h i k l m n o p q r s t v x y
ᗡᏨᏅᏨᏨᎧᏨᎧᏨᎧᏨᎧᏨᎧᏨᎧᏨᎧᏨᎧᏨᎧᏨᎧᏨᎧ

etraſtichon vernacula Vtopienſium lingua.

	ha	Boccas	peu	la
		ᎧᏞᎧᎧᎧᏨ	ᏞᎧᏨᏨᎧ	
	polta		chamaan	
ᎧᏞᎧᎧᎧ		ᎧᎧᎧᎧᎧ		
	he	maglomi		baccan
ᏞᏨᎧᎧ		ᎧᎧᎧᏨᏞᎧᎧ		ᎧᎧᎧᎧᎧ
	gymno	ſophaon		
ᎧᎧᎧᎧᏞ		ᏨᏞᏞᎧᏞᏞ		
	gymnoſophon		labarembacha	

ᎧᎧᎧᏞᏞᏞᏞᏞᏞᎧᎧᎧᎧᎧᎧᎧᎧᎧᎧ
bodamilomin
ᎧᎧᎧᏨᏞᎧᎧᏞ

la	barchin	heman	la
ᎧᏨᎧᎧᎧᎧᎧᏞᎧᎧ		ᎧᎧᎧᎧᏨᎧ	
oluola	dramme		pagloni.
ᏨᏨᏞᏨᎧ	ᎧᎧᎧᎧᎧ		ᏞᎧᎧᏨᏞᏞᎧ

forum verſuum ad verbum hæc eſt ſentencia,
edux ex non inſula fecit inſulam
errarum omnium abſq philoſophia
a philoſophicam expreſſi mortalibus
npartio mea, nõ grauatim accipio meliora,

335

Kateryn Parr, *Prayers and Meditations*

Kateryn's learning and academic achievements were impressive, and in 1545 *Prayers and Meditations* became the first work published by an English queen under her own name.

336

Sir Thomas Elyot, *The Book named the Governor*

A moral and practical treatise on how to be a good Tudor courtier, published in 1531. Elyot had this to say, for example, on the subject of football: 'Nothing but beastily fury and violence, whereof proceed hurt and consequently rancour'. Elyot recommended gentlemen stick to archery and other more noble pursuits.

337

Erasmus, *De Civitate*

As well as being a biblical translator and religious theorist, Erasmus was also an expert on manners. He wrote this book of instructions in 1534. The advice was particularly detailed for dinner party guests: 'Sit not down until you have washed'; 'Place your hands neatly on the table… and not around your belly.'

338

Polydore Vergil, *History of England*

Vergil began his great work at the behest of Henry VII, and completed it in 1533, although it was extended afterwards to cover the whole of Henry VIII's reign.

339

Thomas More, *Utopia*

In 1516, More described a fantasy island state of imagined, although perhaps unreachable, perfection. He invented 'Utopia' from a mixture of Latin and Greek to suggest a place that was both 'good' and 'nowhere'.

340

Anthony Fitzherbert, the *Book of Husbandry*

Fitzherbert was a judge and polymath. In one year (1523) he managed to publish three books: one on law, one on agriculture, and one – rather imaginatively – on law and agriculture. The *Book of Husbandry* was the first practical manual of agricultural technique to be published in England.

Left to right: Holbein's title page for the Coverdale Bible, 1535; Thomas More's *Utopia* and an engraving of Erasmus by Albrecht Dürer, 1526.

Ten (other) 16th-century rulers

Henry was not the only major personality on the globe. Struggles in Europe preoccupied him, but he cannot have been unaware of the activities of rulers further afield, particularly in the Ottoman Empire.

Left to right: A 16th-century map of Europe; Francis I; Suleiman I and Ivan IV – the Terrible.

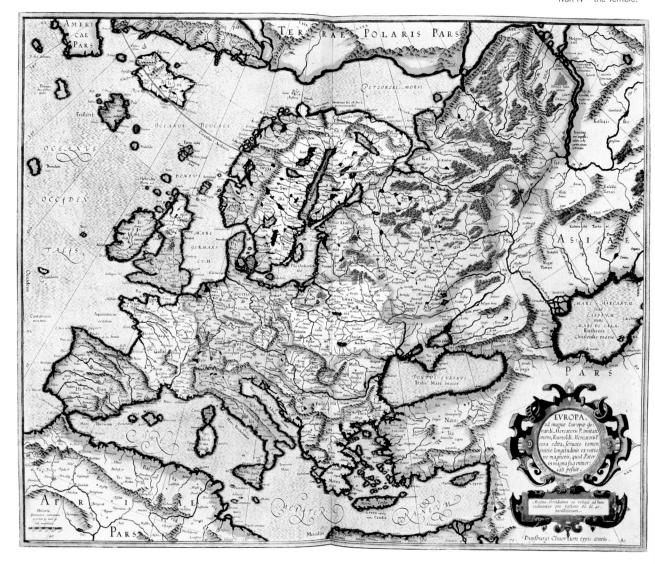

341
Francis I (1515-47)
King of France and Henry VIII's great rival.

342
Isabella (1474-1504) and Ferdinand (1479-1516) of Spain
Parents of Katherine of Aragon and joint rulers of Spain. Responsible for the introduction of the Spanish Inquisition and sponsors of Christopher Columbus's voyages.

343
Maximilian I (1508-19)
Holy Roman Emperor from 1508 until his death. In 1513, he joined forces with Henry VIII to fight the French at the Battle of the Spurs.

344
Charles V (died 1558)
Ruler of the Holy Roman Empire from 1519 and ruler of Spain, as Charles I, from 1516. His son, Philip II, married Henry VIII's daughter, Mary in 1554 in an attempt to make peace between the two countries.

345
Selim I 'the Grim' (1512-20)
Sultan of the Ottoman Empire, he dethroned his father and put his brothers and nephews to death to eliminate pretenders to the throne. He conquered the Middle East and trebled the size of the Empire to nearly 1 billion acres. A poet, he wrote: 'A carpet is large enough to accommodate two sufis, but the world is not large enough for two kings'.

346
Suleiman I (1520-66)
Son of Selim I, Suleiman was the tenth and longest reigning sultan. Known as Suleiman the Magnificent, he travelled west conquering the Christian strongholds of Belgrade, Rhodes and most of Hungary. He presided over a golden age for arts and literature and married the harem girl Roxelena. Suleiman was allied against Henry in 1542, with the Scottish and French.

347
James V (1528-42)
Crowned King of Scotland while still an infant, the country was ruled by a regency for 15 years until James took control in 1528. His mother, Margaret Tudor, was Henry VIII's sister. In 1542 James invaded England but was defeated and died a few weeks later.

348
Babur (1526-31)
Founder of the Moghul Empire, which ruled most of India from 1526 until the mid-18th century.

349
Emperor Go-Nara (1526-57)
105th emperor of Japan but in reality just a figurehead. The country was ruled by great warlords. Oda Nobunga (1534-82) was one of the most powerful.

350
Ivan IV – the Terrible (1530-84)
Grand Prince of Moscow from 1533 and Tsar of all Russia from 1547. He even out did Henry VIII by marrying eight times, sometimes divorcing a week after the wedding. Towards the end of his reign he asked Elizabeth I for asylum in England but died in Russia, possibly poisoned.

Ten world events of Henry's reign

While Henry VIII was ruling England, elsewhere in the world great empires rose and fell, Europeans made their first incursions into the New World and the Reformation divided religious opinion in Europe. These extraordinary events would have cataclysmic consequences for England itself.

Left to right: Martin Luther at the church door in Wittenberg; Magellan's ship, *Victoria,* and *The Siege of Cuzco* by Francisco Pizarro, 1531-2.

THE FIRST SHIP TO CIRCUMNAVIGATE THE WORLD.

351
1517
Martin Luther nails his 95 theses to a church door in Wittenberg, an act which begins the Protestant Reformation.

352
1519
Hernán Cortés arrives in Mexico to begin the conquest of the Aztec empire, which he completes in 1521. Cortés infamously massacres thousands of unarmed native nobility in Cholula, the second largest city in Mexico, before marching on Tenochtitlan. The Aztec Emperor, Moctezuma, peacefully delivers the capital city to the conquistador, believing Cortés to be the god Quetzalcoatl himself.

353
1519-22
The first round the world trip! A Spanish expedition led by Ferdinand Magellan is the first to circle the globe. Magellan himself was killed during a fight with natives in the Philippine Islands in April 1521, and only one ship and 18 men completed the circumnavigation.

354
1520
Suleiman the Magnificent becomes Emperor of the Ottoman Empire. This tremendous empire covered Turkey, Egypt, Greece, Bulgaria, Hungary, Palestine, Romania, Jordan, Lebanon and Syria at the height of its power.

355
1524-5
300,000 German peasants join in a huge popular uprising known as the Peasant's War. They are eventually crushed and 100,000 are estimated to have lost their lives.

356
1526
The Moghul empire is established in India, by Babur. The Moghuls rule India until 1739.

357
1527
Rome is sacked and pillaged by the troops of Charles V, the Holy Roman Emperor. Pope Clement VIII is imprisoned.

358
1532
The Spanish mount another Latin American invasion – this time Francisco Pizarro marches into Peru to conquer the Incas.

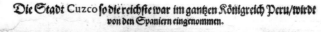

359
1534-5
The German city of Münster is the site of a radical Anabaptist attempt to establish a theocracy, which lasts for 18 months. Polygamy is legalized, all property is held in common, and the Anabaptists call Münster 'the new Jerusalem'. When the town is recaptured in 1535, the Anabaptists are tortured to death and their bodies displayed in cages.

360
1541
The Amazon river is discovered by the Spanish explorer Francisco de Orellana. Despite threatened mutiny and attack from hostile natives, de Orellana sails the length of the river.

361

Salisbury

This and other cathedral cities were among the largest centres of urban population and prosperity throughout the 16th century. The cathedral close and surrounding streets, planned as a medieval new town, still give a sense of what the city was like in early Tudor times, and the Doom painting in St Thomas's church is a vivid reminder of pre-Reformation religious belief.

362

London

Always the largest city, but at some 50,000 London was the size of a present-day country town. Almost wholly contained within the ancient walls that still constitute the Square Mile of the City of London, the metropolis was filled with parish churches, monasteries, livery company halls, manufacturers and traders. To the west, the royal centre of Westminster was still a tiny settlement, to the east the Tower of London marked the edge of the built-up area. The Great Fire of 1666 swept away much of the old city, although pockets of medieval and Tudor London survive.

363

Norwich

With perhaps 10,000 people Norwich was, until the 18th century, the second city in England. Its dozens of churches, often rebuilt and enhanced in the years around 1500, stand as testimony to the wealth of Norwich, founded upon the East Anglian wool trade.

364

Bristol

This was slightly smaller than Norwich, and it too remained one of the largest

A view of Salisbury Cathedral.
Right: Thomas Wolsey, who was created Archbishop of York in 1514, by an unknown artist, *c*1520.
Far right: The parish church of Lavenham.

Ten important towns of Henry VIII's England

In contrast to many European countries, English towns had little power, their medieval heydays were over and urban economies were in crisis. Yet enough survives to give a sense of the scale and value of urban settings.

provincial centres until the 18th century. Bristol's wealth and status largely stemmed from the sea, and increasingly from the Atlantic trades (and Bristol men may well have 'discovered' America before Columbus).

365
Newcastle
This was one of only two major urban centres in the north of England. The coal trade, which underpinned the city's wealth in later years, was just beginning to take hold; the city had a strategic importance close to the border with Scotland and acted as a major regional centre.

366
York
With 7,000 to 8,000 inhabitants York probably matched Newcastle in size and scale, but its medieval glory days were fast diminishing as its industrial base waned. The number of medieval churches, the close-set streets, and the grandeur of the Minster church all indicate the former prosperity and regional importance of York.

367
King's Lynn
This town was called Bishop's Lynn until the Reformation, when the power over it was taken from the Bishop of Norwich and given to the Crown. One of the major ports on the east coast, King's Lynn still boasts some spectacular surviving buildings from the early Tudor era.

368
Shrewsbury
This was one of a number of towns with some 4,000 to 5,000 inhabitants. Almost encircled by the River Severn, the town stood as a gateway to Wales and the border country. Like other urban centres, it had fallen on hard times by 1500 with industrial decline. The town regained importance as a market and trading centre a century or so later.

369
Exeter
Although badly bombed in the Second World War, when many of its great surviving Tudor buildings were destroyed, sufficient remains to indicate the wealth and self-importance of Devon's premier town.

370
Lavenham
This is the odd town out. It was much smaller, probably only a thousand people or so, but in the 1520s taxation lists it was one of the richest settlements in England. Today, its early Tudor houses make it a remarkable showpiece. The cloth industry in the town accounts for much of the wealth – and Lavenham survives so little-altered because it went almost immediately into swift, near-terminal industrial decline.

Ten innovations of Henry's reign

The world in Tudor times was getting more convenient, more luxurious and more high-tech. Some of the most exciting innovations from the Tudor period now seem rather quaint, but others remain with us today.

371

In 1544 Henry VIII devalued the English coinage – so he can be said to have invented inflation! He did it to get more money to fund his fight with the French. In 1562, after Henry's death, his debased silver coins had to be withdrawn from circulation.

372

Under Henry, the English navy was built up from five to about 40 ships – its biggest yet. Among various improvements the 'gunport' was invented. These little doors in the sides of warships allowed the new and larger cannons to be fired during sea battles.

373

Henry walked on the first kind of fitted carpet! Previously rushes were strewn loose on the palace floors, and had to be taken away and replaced every week, until an enterprising person sewed rushes together in strips to make a more permanent kind of floor covering. A piece of Tudor rush matting was found underneath the floorboards at Hampton Court Palace in the 1990s.

374

Fixed four-poster beds first appeared in Henry VIII's reign. Before that there were tester beds, with a canopy suspended from the walls and ceiling rather than being integral to the bed,

Above: Breech-loading wheel-lock gun made for Henry VIII, *c*1537. *From left to right:* 16th-century coins bearing the likeness of Henry VIII; *The Embarkation of Henry VIII at Dover* (detail) showing gunports in the King's warships; a 16th-century fork (prongs and handle); terracotta roundel from Hampton Court; the Great Bed of Ware, *c*1590.

or demountable four-posters like the replica of Edward I's on display at the Tower of London. Headboards from beds for Anne of Cleves (see page 100) and Anne Boleyn survive in the Burrell Collection, Glasgow, and at Hever Castle respectively.

375

Terracotta antique-style decoration, some of which can still be seen on great houses today, first arrived in England during Henry's lifetime. Cardinal Wolsey had already commissioned roundels for Hampton Court, and other forms of this decoration from the Italian Renaissance began to prove popular among the wealthy.

376

Henry's physician, Thomas Linacre, introduced the Damask rose to England. The Damask rose had been known in mainland Europe since the Middle Ages when crusaders returning from Damascus brought it with them. This rose's great advantage was that it flowered more than once in a season. It was picked early in the morning to harvest the essential oil in its petals.

377

Did Henry launch gun culture? The King was very keen on firearms and created his own experimental weapons foundry in 1511. Small personal weapons like the pistol also began to be popular among his subjects, so the first laws controlling their use were passed in Henry's reign.

378

The secret of creating porcelain, known for centuries in China, was developed in Venice from about 1470, and Henry VIII owned at least three of these newly-fashionable 'pots of earth, painted, called porcelain'.

379

Henry actually had a tap in his bathroom! Although medieval monks had been expert at providing running water to their monasteries, Hampton Court Palace is unusual for its complicated but effective system of brick conduits, which brought water from Coombe Conduit three miles away.

380

A new Italian implement called the forchette – fork – began to appear in Henry's palaces at mealtimes. The new-fangled, highly decorated fork was probably only used by the King himself or possibly for serving slices of meat. Diners still used their own personal knives and their fingers, with maybe a spoon for pottage.

Henry VIII (detail)
by Hans Holbein
the Younger, 1536.

HENRY'S IMAGE

❀

Henry VIII is probably the first English monarch who can be instantly recognised, in an image created by Hans Holbein the Younger. Much copied – even on film – this image has stayed with us ever since. The 'greatest' Tudor monarch, dazzling us with his own magnificent confidence. But there are many negatives about Henry and many other portraits of this flawed colossus. Who was the real Henry?

Ten Henry clichés: true, false or simply unfair?

So you think that Henry VIII was fat, over-sexed and had anger management issues? Dig about a bit behind the clichés and a more complex but more interesting truth will always emerge...

glory'. The other side of his rages were extremes of physical affection; ambassador Chapuys, for example, described how, in 1535, the king 'put his hands around my neck and walked for some time with me'. In later life, however, Henry grew increasingly paranoid. His divorce from Katherine of Aragon left him 'so troubled in his brain about this matter that he does not trust any one alive'. Only in later years, many executions behind him, was he described by one of his courtiers as 'the most dangerous and cruel man in the world'.

381
Henry was over-sexed
UNFAIR Well, even setting aside his relationships with the Boleyn girls, there were certainly rumours enough that the King was 'of amorous complexion'; that he wanted 'only an apple and a fair wench to dally with'; that he was 'given to matters of dancing and of ladies'; that he was 'continually inclined to amours'. But hard evidence of extreme promiscuity is more difficult to find and, indeed, he waited six or seven years before sleeping with Anne Boleyn. The accusations are just part of Henry VIII's growing unpopularity as his reign wore on. See page 28 for his complete (and small) list of mistresses.

382
Henry VIII was a thug, prizing brawn above brain
FALSE Henry was fluent in French, in battle strategy, in theology. He was fascinated by astromony, and would spend hours in discussion with Sir Thomas More, sometimes even going up on to the roofs of his palaces with More to gaze at the heavens.

383
He was always angry
UNFAIR Yes, he could explode, but sometimes in his youth it was staged as a tool for diplomacy, or to show who was in charge. The Italian philosopher Niccolò Machiavelli, for example, called him 'rich, ferocious and eager for

384
Henry stole Hampton Court Palace from Cardinal Wolsey
UNFAIR It's not as clear cut as that. Henry often stayed at Hampton Court Palace when it was indisputably Cardinal Wolsey's, but the King gradually began to use the palace more, and eventually asked Wolsey to leave.

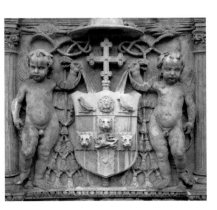

385
Henry preferred sport and leisure to work – and let Wolsey run the country
UNFAIR Henry did love to spent most of the day hunting and socialising. However, although he was not inclined to business, the King could reveal in a flash that he knew exactly what had been going on in the world of politics. In the words of his biographer JJ Scarisbrick, Henry VIII could: 'time and again, show a detailed grasp of foreign affairs and hold his own with, if not outdo, foreign ambassadors'. He could 'suddenly put off his supper until he had dealt with a stack of business… pounce on something Wolsey had missed… cut a proposal to ribbons with a few swift strokes… assess a situation exactly… confidently overrule his minister… correctly predict that a plan could not work'.

386
Henry was very fat
TRUE but only towards the end of his life. In his younger years he was extremely handsome and very slender for such a tall man. In 1536, the year that an unpleasant fall ended his jousting career, the King's armourers found that his waist measured 89cm (35in). In his fifties, though, after his miserable trials with Catherine Howard and a bout of comfort eating, his waist measured 137cm (54in). 'Marvellous excess' in food and wine was to blame.

387
Henry wasn't very fat
TRUE From around 2006 there was a new fashion for overturning the gross old stereotype of Henry. There has been a spate of popular depictions of Henry showing him as forever young and sexy – and with it a new cliché was born. Enjoy a slim, handsome Henry in the film *The Other Boleyn Girl*, the TV series 'The Tudors', and the *Young Henry VIII* exhibition at Hampton Court Palace.

388
Henry created the Protestant church in England
FALSE Until his death Henry VIII still considered himself to be a Catholic, and he heard the Latin Mass all his life. He wasn't keen on Protestants with their doctrine of 'justification by faith' rather than by doing good works. 'It was merry in England afore the New Learning came up', he said towards the end of his life. 'Yea, I would all things were as hath been in times past'.

389
Henry had red hair
TRUE His beard came and went, though.

390
Henry wrote the tune 'Greensleeves'
FALSE? Often claimed, never definitively proved.

From left to right: Scene from *The Private Life of Henry VIII,* 1933; *Astronomicum Caesareum* by Apianus, 1540 – one of Henry's many books on astronomy; scene from George Cavendish's *The Life of Wolsey*; Wolsey's coat of arms at Hampton Court; Eric Bana as a slim Henry VIII in *The Other Boleyn Girl,* 2008.

Henry on film

From East End gangster to victim of manipulative women, sensitive soul to ludicrous lothario, portrayals of Henry on large and small screens say as much about our perceptions of the King as the actors' interpretation. Here are ten actors who brought Henry alive for mass audiences.

391

Arthur Bourchier – *Henry VIII* (1911) dir. William G B Barker
This short, silent production, based on a part of Shakespeare's play of the same name was the first film about Henry VIII. It also starred Sir Herbert Beerbohm Tree as Wolsey.

392

Charles Laughton – *The Private Life of Henry VIII* (1933), dir. Alexander Korda. Also starring Merle Oberon, Elsa Lanchester and Robert Donat
Laughton's Henry is a likeable, sympathetic character at the mercy of manipulative women. He is vulnerable and sentimental, as well as blustery and vulgar, and is portrayed as a lonely, wronged man. However, he is also 'immature, awkward, comically embarrassed by the prospect of sex, when in the company of desirable… women', according to scholar Greg Walker.

393

Richard Burton – *Anne of the Thousand Days* (1969), dir. Charles Jarrott. Also starring Genevieve Bujold, Anthony Quayle and Michael Hordern
Perhaps unsurprisingly, the great British thespian played a good-looking, suave, masculine and flamboyant hero-king. No waddling here – Henry/Burton is a slim, ageless lover, resplendent in every scene. The film is notable too for the oft-quoted line: 'divorce is like killing – after the first time, it's easy'.

**Robert Shaw – *A Man for All Seasons*
(1966), dir. Fred Zinnemann and
based on the play by Robert Bolt.
Also starring Paul Scofield, Orson
Welles and Susannah York**

Although the central character of this
fine film is Henry's Lord Chancellor
Sir Thomas More (played by Scofield),
the personality of the King looms large
over the action. Shaw's Henry is a
believably flawed man rather than
monstrous monarch, switching from
laughter to wild rage and keeping
courtiers on tenterhooks.

**Keith Michell – 'The Six Wives of
Henry VIII' (BBC TV series, 1971)**

In this immensely popular series, each
differently-authored episode featured
a wife, and a gradually expanding
and increasingly bearded Henry. It
was a mainly sympathetic portrayal,
with Michell saying (in the *Radio
Times*, January 1971) that the King's
alleged sexual proclivities tended to
overshadow his achievements and
intellect, adding the classic comment
'I sometimes wonder if he had any
more relationships with women than
ordinary men today. The fact that he
married them all just made it that much
more apparent.'

396

id James – *Carry on Henry* (1971),
ir. Gerald Thomas. Also starring
Kenneth Williams and Barbara
Windsor.

n best Carry On tradition, Sid
ames pulls out all the stops to play a
udicrous, rash and randy Henry, intent
n bedding and beheading. Most of
ne film concentrates on his efforts
o remove his garlic-loving queen;
ne, enjoyably, manages to thwart the
ttempts on her life.

397

Philippe Rouillon – *Henri VIII*
(1991), dir. Pierre Jourdan. Also
starring Michèle Command, Lucile
Vignon and Alain Gabriel.

Henry sings… this opera in four parts,
written by Camille Saint-Saens is
based on Shakespeare's play, set in the
early life of Henry VIII as he divorces
Katherine of Aragon. It was revived in
1991 in a production starring the French
baritone Rouillon, who also took the
lead role in a film of the opera.

398

Ray Winstone – *Henry VIII* (TV film,
Granada, 2003), dir. Pete Travis.
Also starring Helena Bonham Carter
and David Suchet.

'This is *The Godfather* in tights'
promised the director, and hard guy
actor Ray Winstone played Henry as
the 'gangster king', with a few tender
love scenes juxtaposed with a fictitious
brutal rape. Winstone described Henry
as 'probably the biggest gangster of
them all' and kept his East End accent
to prove it.

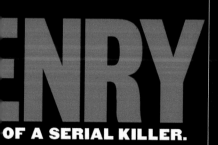

ENRY

OF A SERIAL KILLER.

IS HENRY VIII. COMING SOON.

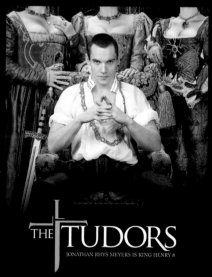

THE TUDORS
JONATHAN RHYS MEYERS IS KING HENRY 8

Natalie Portman Scarlett Johansson Eric Bana

the
other Boleyn girl

THE ONLY THING THAT COULD COME BETWEEN THESE SISTERS...
IS A KINGDOM.

BASED ON THE BEST SELLING NOVEL

399

Jonathan Rhys Meyers – *The Tudors* (2007), created by Michael Hirst. Also starring Henry Cavill, Natalie Dormer, Jeremy Northam and Sam Neill.

Sexy, although a bit on the small side (Henry was 6ft 2in) Rhys Meyers lives up to Henry's reputation as the 'handsomest prince in Christendom'. This American-made television series, with plenty of heaving bosoms, luscious costumes and oodles of dramatic licence challenged the stereotype of old, fat Henry. Lusty, fit and energetic, Rhys Meyers evoked a young Henry VIII.

400

Eric Bana – *The Other Boleyn Girl* (2008), dir. Justin Chadwick and based on the book by Philippa Gregory. Also starring Natalie Portman and Scarlett Johansson.

Bana makes a physically impressive and charismatic younger Henry, although the limelight is stolen by the manipulative (and manipulated) Anne Boleyn and her more docile sister, Mary. Although we glimpse his private anguish over divorce and desperate desire for an heir, Henry's character is less interesting than the power struggles that surge around him at court as the über-ambitious Thomas Boleyn pimps both his daughters to the King.

From left to right:
Portraits of Henry, all
painted by unknown
artists; Henry VIII
(detail), c1509; Henry
VIII as a child; Henry
VIII, c1509 and Henry
VIII, c1520.

Henry captured

It is often claimed that Holbein's iconic portrait is Henry VIII; that it is somehow a reflection of the personality of the man himself. But what about all the other images of Henry that are often overlooked?

401
The little Prince
Before Henry the man, there was Henry the child – a little prince who we first meet delighting his parents at the wedding feast of his older brother, dancing with his sister Margaret. Little Henry was cocky and charismatic certainly, but not – yet – the brutal bully of the 1540s.

402
Young Henry
When he came to the throne in 1509, Henry was young, athletic and handsome. He was a leader of men who took his knightly prowess to the battlefields of Flanders and whipped the armies of the withered syphilitic French King, Louis XII. He was the 'handsomest potentate' the Venetian ambassador had ever set eyes on.

403
Henry in his prime
At the Field of Cloth of Gold in 1520, Henry presided over a Renaissance court at one of the most glitteringly extravagant royal parties every thrown. It is surely a mistake to think that the rest of Henry's reign – the food, the women, the executions – was somehow inevitable at this point.

404
Updating Henry

Henry's personality and his image developed as the 1520s turned into the 1530s. Portraits were even repainted to keep up with changing fashions: it was important, it seems, to have the most recent Henry on your walls at home, to show you were still in touch with the times.

405
Henry in miniature

Hans Holbein wasn't the highest paid artist at the Tudor court. Lucas Horenbout was paid more money than his younger protégée, and executed this tiny jewel-like miniature portrait of Henry. The Horenbout family's portraits of the mid-1520s are the earliest miniature paintings in England.

406
Henry Inc.

It is too often assumed that this was the image of Henry that everyone knew at the time, just like they do today. It wasn't. Holbein's original small-scale portrait was probably a private commission, used as a gift. No prints of this image were issued in Henry's lifetime, so it was far from being some sort of brand, or approved image, that the King consciously circulated.

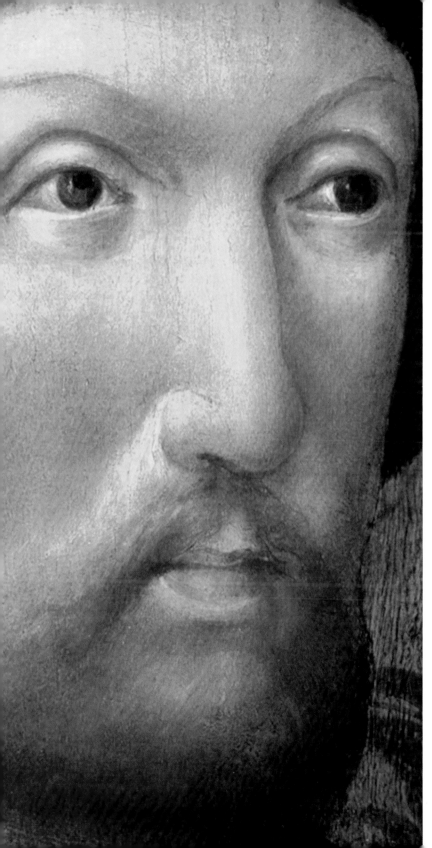

407
Big Henry

Holbein did, admittedly, also paint a life-size Henry across the wall of his Privy Chamber in Whitehall Palace. This was still not a public image, but copies from this portrait were commissioned during Henry's lifetime, by local courtiers and institutions that benefited from Henry's patronage.

From left to right: Portrait and x-ray photograph of *Henry VIII*, early 16th century; miniature of the King by Lucas Horenbout; Holbein's famous portrait of Henry VIII (detail) dated 1536; Henry VIII (detail) by an unknown artist, *c*1520; Cartoon for the *Whitehall Mural* (detail) by Hans Holbein the Younger, 1537.

408
Henry as Solomon
This is how Henry probably most liked to see himself. As some sort of post-Biblical patriarch, leading his people to a new promised land, away from the disobliging Church of Rome. Here, Henry – again painted by Holbein – appears as King Solomon; elsewhere Henry stars as Abraham and David.

409
Henry the old and fat
This is a Henry who, by the 1540s, has been damaged, both physically and psychologically, by his failed European policies, by his defeats abroad and in the marriage bed, by being made a cuckold and by being reduced to a limping parody of the young athletic prince.

410
Henry the 21st-century celebrity
Jonathan Rhys Meyers as Henry VIII, from 'The Tudors', 2007. This is Henry VIII du jour, a popstar from the pages of *Hello!* magazine, with Anne Boleyn drapped across his bed like a footballer's wife in a photoshoot. After centuries of being known by Holbein's portrait, Henry is probably sitting around, watching, saying to himself, 'About time!'

From left to right: Henry VIII (detail) after Hans Holbein the Younger, *late 16th century; Solomon and the Queen of Sheba* by Hans Holbein the Younger, *c1535; Henry VIII* after Hans Holbein the Younger, *late 16th century;* Jonathan Rhys Meyers and Natalie Dormer as Henry VIII and Anne Boleyn.

Hotpants depicting Henry VIII designed by Betty Jackson.

HENRY'S LEGACY

✿

Henry VIII slept here. Henry VIII hunted here. Henry VIII found a wife here. The memories of place and time linger. Henry VIII also has more tangible legacies. His children are among them, notably Queen Elizabeth I, a close contender for the title of greatest monarch. The establishment of a separate English church has a claim to be one of the most crucial events in the nation's long history, together with the English Bible that embodied the replacement of ecclesiastical authority by royal authority and the authorised land grab that transformed wealth and topography. Above all, it is the image of Henry VIII that persists, a king who was larger than life.

How Henry changed the way we live today

Five centuries later, the actions of one Tudor monarch still have an impact on our lives. Some – Henry's support of medical science – have been beneficial. Others such as his discriminatory laws, have left a darker legacy.

411
Religion

Henry VIII created the Church of England. The action of breaking from Rome and establishing himself as the Supreme Head of the Church of England declared to the world that no foreign ruler would ever again have authority over England, and helped create a new sense of English national identity. Henry was also the first English king to authorise the translation and publication of the Bible in English, allowing all people access to a fundamental religious text in their own language. He ordered that an English Bible be put in every parish church in the land.

412
Land ownership

Henry VIII oversaw the dissolution of the monasteries, which changed the religious and architectural face of Britain. The destruction of monastic buildings was of huge architectural consequence. The sale of monastic property created a land market in England, enriching a new British aristocracy.

413
The modern state

Henry promoted parliamentary government by extending representation and expanding the privileges of both houses. He also overhauled the machinery of the state by introducing progressive and efficient tax schemes, and substantial new governmental bureaucracy.

414
Uniting the kingdom

Henry VIII formally annexed Wales to England in 1536 and 1543, and established the counties of Wales; the border has remained the same ever since. He was also the first English king to attempt to subdue and rule Ireland. Scotland, however, eluded him.

415
The English navy

Henry was the principal founder of the English navy. The fleet of warships he built was the first standing military force of its time, and the basis for Britain's future dominance of the seas. His navy was key to England's later victory over the Spanish Armada, and allowed the development of English colonies overseas. He also invested greatly in shipbuilding, dockyards, innovations like cannons, and defensive fortresses along the south coast, such as Dover and Walmer castles.

416
Discrimination

Henry introduced several laws that curtailed personal freedom and punished 'difference'. The first law against witchcraft was passed in 1542, which was to have huge consequences over the next two centuries in the persecution of witches (who were mainly women). The Buggery Act brought homosexual activity into the courts, and to the scaffold.

417
Arts and medicine

Henry VIII patronised innovation in both the arts and medical sciences. He employed Hans Holbein as his court painter and oversaw the setting up of the Royal College of Physicians in 1518 (the first legislation of medical practice), the Barber-Surgeons' Charter of 1541, and the so-called 'Quacks' Charter' which has provided a legal standing for herbalists ever since.

418
Women in power

Henry VIII was the father of England's first two queens-regnant and secured the Tudor dynasty.

419
Respect!

Henry asserted a place for England on the international stage when it was a small, minor country. Swaggering on, he demanded respect for England in the eyes of his contemporaries (the King of France, Francis I and the Holy Roman Emperor, Charles V). He gained an elevated status for England that has never been fully diminished.

420
Symbol of Britain

Henry VIII's iconic image and legend have become embedded in the national consciousness. The magnificence and proud splendour of this monarch remain an important part of notions of Britishness.

Ten surviving palaces and houses

At the height of his reign, Henry owned, or used scores of palaces, great houses and castles. Many whole, or partial survivals can be visited today.

421
Hampton Court Palace, Surrey

Henry's most famous residence, a palace devoted to pleasure, celebration and ostentatious display. When Henry finished his building programme in around 1540, Hampton Court was the most modern, sophisticated and magnificent palace in England. All of Henry's six wives came to the palace and most had new and lavish lodgings. The King rebuilt his own rooms at least half a dozen times.

422
St James's Palace, Westminster, London

Henry built this palace on the site of St James's hospital. Anne Boleyn spent the night after her coronation here, and the entwined initials H and A can be seen carved into a couple of the fireplaces. Henry Fitzroy, the King's illegitimate son was living here when he died in 1536 aged 17. Much survives of Henry's red-brick palace, including the Chapel Royal, the gatehouse and two Tudor rooms in the Royal Apartments. It is not open to the public.

423
Hatfield Palace (now Hatfield House), Hertfordshire

The original palace was built by the Bishop of Ely in around 1485, and Henry acquired it with the dispersal of Church possessions. He used it chiefly as a residence for his three children, and the house is mainly associated with Princess Elizabeth, who spent her childhood here with Edward, and later less happily as a virtual prisoner of her sister Queen Mary. It was at Hatfield that Elizabeth learnt of her accession to the throne in 1558. One side of the original building containing the banqueting house still stands to the west of the house.

424
Windsor Castle, Berkshire

The oldest and largest occupied castle in the world, Windsor played host to Henry and his court on many occasions. He is buried with his beloved third wife, Jane Seymour, in St George's Chapel.

425
Eltham Palace, London

The great medieval hall, part of Henry's childhood home and built by his grandfather Edward IV, survives next to the fabulous 1930s Art Deco mansion built by textile magnates Stephen and Virginia Courtauld. It was a favoured place of retreat early in Henry's reign. The Eltham Ordinances of 1518 were the codification of court organisation and etiquette, and all at court had to abide by these rules.

Clockwise from top left:
Hampton Court Palace,
the Tower of London,
Leeds Castle, St James's
Palace.

426
The Tower of London

Henry expanded the royal residences at the Tower, commissioning a large range of timber-framed buildings for the comfort and enjoyment of his second wife Anne Boleyn, who was executed there three years later. After this time Henry's chief use of the Tower was to incarcerate many political and religious prisoners, and as a fortress and mighty arsenal.

427
Leeds Castle, Maidstone, Kent

This 12th-century castle was visited frequently by Henry, most notably with his first queen Katherine of Aragon and their court *en route* to the tournament the Field of Cloth of Gold in France.

428
Acton Court, Iron Acton, Bristol

Today, Her Majesty Queen Elizabeth II can expect the places she stays to be spruced up in her honour. In 1535, in anticipation of a visit from Henry VIII and Anne Boleyn, courtier Sir Nicholas Poyntz tore down his kitchen block and built a range of luxury apartments! A court report of a four-month royal progress in 1535 by the King and Queen records that the couple spent a long weekend there in August. The house was purchased by English Heritage in 1985.

429
Dartford Manor House, Kent

After the dissolution of the monastries, Henry built a series of houses on the road from London to the coast as places to stay on his regular journeys south and also to accommodate distinguished foreign visitors. The King chose sites at Dartford, Rochester and Canterbury; at Dartford this involved the demolition of all buildings connected with Dartford Priory. In June 1545, Dartford's Royal Manor House became the venue for a series of meetings of the Privy Council. Anne of Cleves lived at the Manor House between 1553 and 1557. Part of Henry's Manor House is still standing, owned by Dartford Borough Council.

430
Hunsdon House, Hunsdonbury, Herfortshire

Sir William Oldham built the original house of brick in 1447 in the form of a tower. In around 1525 Henry developed the original building into a great Tudor house with a moat. A gatehouse and summer house still survive. The palatial house can be glimpsed in the background of a portrait of Prince Edward painted in 1536. The house was largely a residence for the King's three children. Legend says that it was here that Princess Mary taught her younger sister Elizabeth to play cards.

Raise your glasses to Henry!

Possibly the most famous pub named after the King is next to Hever Castle, but many other pubs in the south and London area proudly claim links to this most famous monarch, mixed with a good measure of myth perhaps!

431
King Henry VIII Inn, Hever Road Hever, Kent
Situated in the little village of Hever, next to Hever Castle, childhood home of Anne Boleyn.

432
Great Harry, Woolwich, London SE18
This pub is named after Henry's warship, the *Great Harry*, built in Woolwich in 1512-14.

433
The Lamb – Lamb's Conduit Street, London WC1
The pub name comes from William Lamb, a Gentleman of the Chapel Royal of Henry VIII. A water conduit was built there in 1498 and Lamb improved it at his own expense in 1577.

434
The Black Friar, Queen Victoria Street, London E1
The Dominican order or Black Friars founded a monastery here in the 13th century, that was closed down at the dissolution of the monastries in 1538. In 1596, actor James Burbage bought the land and built Blackfriars Theatre. And what was the first play ever staged there? Shakespeare's *Henry VIII*.

435
Old King's Head, King's Head Yard, London SE1
This pub was originally known as The Pope's Head. After Henry's falling out with His Holiness, the diplomatic pub owner swiftly changed the name!

436
Spotted Dog Inn, Upton Lane, E7
While still married to Katherine of Aragon, Henry liked to visit Anne Boleyn at nearby Westham Palace while he was out hunting with his dogs. There is a large plaster statue of Henry and the spotted dog inside.

437
Prospect of Whitby, Wapping Wall, London E1
Built in 1520, this ancient London pub was constructed at the same time Henry met Francis I at the Field of Cloth of Gold.

438
Old Nun's Head, Nunhead Green, London SW15
This was first licensed in the reign of Henry VIII. The pub was built on the site of a nunnery suppressed by the King. One local tale is that the rather beautiful Mother Superior had been caught kissing Henry and she was murdered to keep her quiet!

439
Queen's Head and Artichoke, London NW1
This was named after Henry's younger sister Mary, wife of Louis XII of France.

440
The Old King's Head, Hampton Court Road, Surrey
A mile down the road from Hampton Court Palace and at the end of a pleasant walk through Home Park, Henry's old hunting ground, is this public house where our most famous Tudor monarch is toasted still.

'Tudor' drinkers at
Hampton Court Palace.
Left: Pub sign from
The Old King's Head,
London.

Ten fabulous survivals from Henry's reign

These objects, which throw a light on some of the fabulous things Henry had at court, still exist, and can be seen today.

441
Katherine of Aragon's writing desk
This rare writing desk may have been made for Henry VIII or Katherine of Aragon. It is decorated with Henry's coat of arms, the initials 'H' and 'K' and Katherine's sheaf of arrows symbol. The desk would have held paper and writing equipment.

442
Anne Boleyn's clock
Supposedly given to the Queen by Henry VIII in 1533. The two weights inside the clock are engraved with the letters 'H' and 'A', with lovers' knots and the mottoes of Henry and Anne.

443

The Abraham tapestries

Commissioned by Henry VIII in the 1540s, probably for the Great Hall at Hampton Court where they still hang, the Abraham tapestries were woven with real silver and gold thread and were one of the most expensive sets commissioned by the King. By his death in 1547, Henry had amassed over 2,000 tapestries. Fewer than 30 survive today.

444

The *Mary Rose*

This magnificent warship was the pride of Henry's fleet but sank in the Solent during an engagement with the French fleet on 19 July 1545. The ship was raised from the seabed in 1982 and is on public display in Portsmouth Historic Dockyard.

445

Illuminated manuscript

This exquisite illuminated manuscript from Henry's library, which survives at the British Library, was a gift to the King and is decorated with the royal arms. The volume contains Collenuccio's *Apologues* and Lucian's *Dialogues*.

446

The Royal Clock Salt
A gift to Henry VIII from Francis I, this ostentatious piece of tableware is one of only three pieces of plate known to have survived from Henry's jewel house. The base originally contained a clock mechanism and the salt was held **in a well above the hexagonal section.**

447

Holbein's designs for jewellery
During her short reign as queen, Jane Seymour was showered with gifts of jewellery from her besotted husband. Designs for some of the most elaborate pieces, with Henry and Jane's initials entwined together, survive at the British Museum.

448

Henry's sword
Made for Henry VIII in 1544 by Diego da Caias, this iron and gold hunting sword is decorated with hunting scenes and a depiction of Henry's siege of Boulogne in 1544. The blade is inscribed in Latin, celebrating the King's victory over the French.

449
Royal gold cup
Made of solid gold and decorated with enamels depicting the life and miracles of St Agnes, this elaborate French cup dates from c1370-80, but was later owned by Henry VIII.

450
Barber-Surgeon's instrument case
This lavishly decorated case for holding surgical instruments was made in about 1520-25 and was possibly a gift from Henry VIII to a royal surgeon. Made of silver, parcelgilt and enamel, it is decorated with the arms of the King and those of the Barber-Surgeon's Company.

What Henry means to me...

Like him or loathe him?
Henry VIII 500 Facts *authors reveal their personal views*

451

Lucy Worsley, Chief Curator

It's easy to think of Henry VIII as the terrible monster of his paranoid old age, but he was once a little boy full of charm and hope. I think that in many ways being thrust into the role of monarch – had his brother lived, he wouldn't have inherited the throne – places a terrible burden on the human being affected. By the 1540s Henry VIII was old, bloated, weary and guilty, but I prefer to remember him as a little boy laughing: before his became the uneasy head that wears the crown.

452

Lee Prosser, Curator (Historic Buildings)

Henry dazzled his adoring subjects with pageantry, spectacle and naked power with such skill that some of it has rubbed off on us. Were we to stand with the Venetian ambassador, would we not also swoon at the sight of this tall, strapping, golden-haired youth with so much promise? Why do I admire him? Because for all the ugly characteristics of the ageing, gout-ridden, petulant old man, England needed a strong ruler to prevent her from slipping back into the endless, ruinous civil wars of the past, to snap the bonds of the Papacy, advance men of ruthless efficiency and skill, and bring forth the nation state. Henry helped make the modern world, and few characters from history have embedded themselves so deeply in our national consciousness.

453
Suzannah Lipscomb, Research Curator

Henry was a man of intense feeling, but little emotional intelligence, wilful and obstinate, but also charming and charismatic, he had a profound sense of responsibility to fulfil his divinely ordained role. From the halcyon days of his youth, when he had been successful at everything he turned his hand to, his life was marked by gradual decline and frustration. A great series of losses and misadventures created anxiety and insecurity in him, and in the latter part of his life, the actions of some of those close to him produced a terrible sense of betrayal which in turn led to self-justification and aggression. His sadness and savage rage could be devastating, but he was, above all, a proud, awesome and well-intentioned, if also a flawed and self-deceiving, monarch.

454
Brett Dolman, Curator (Collections)

Henry VIII was a vicious, paranoid, self-pitying, vainglorious, workshy philanderer and spendthrift. Everything he did was to further his own bank balance or self-importance, and he mostly did not care what or who stood in his way and nothing was ever his fault. He failed in the marriage bed, on the battlefield and at the negotiating table. There is almost nothing redeeming about his character or his actions, although as a consequence of his blinkered and self-serving approach to politics and marriage, some rather important changes were effected during his reign, not least the establishment of the Church of England. We remain fascinated by him, largely on the basis of his brutishness and the fact that he executed two of his wives.

455
David Souden, Head of Access and Learning

Henry VIII was the English Stalin.

Twelve great books

Read even more about Henry!

His palaces

456

Hampton Court: A Social and Architectural History, Simon Thurley
(Yale University Press, 2003)

457

Hampton Court Palace: The Official Illustrated History, Lucy Worsley and David Souden
(Merrell, 2005)

458

Royal Palaces of Tudor England: Architecture and Court Life, 1460-1547, Simon Thurley
(Yale University Press, 1993)

459

The Royal Palaces of London, David Souden
(Merrell, 2008)

460

The Tower of London: The Official Illustrated History, Edward Impey and Geoffrey Parnell
(Merrell, 2000)

The man, his life and wives

461

Great Harry, The Extravagant Life of Henry VIII, Carolly Erickson
(Robson Books, 2004)

462

Henry VIII, JJ Scarisbrick
(Yale University Press, 1997)

463

Henry VIII, King and Court, Alison Weir
(Pimlico, 2002)

464

Henry: Virtuous Prince, David Starkey
(HarperPress, 2008)

465

Six Wives of Henry VIII, Antonia Fraser
(Phoenix, 2002)

466

Henry's Blog, Elizabeth Newbery
(Historic Royal Palaces, 2009)

467

Henry VIII, Manga Shakespeare
(SelfMadeHero, 2009)

Henry slept here (and in some places, you can too!)

Henry VIII was a peripatetic king, moving from palace to palace, as whim (and cleaning requirements) dictated. When he wasn't staying at one of his own residences, he expected richer members of the court to play host.

Bedroom at Hever Castle

468
The Tower of London
Henry stayed at the Tower on the night before his coronation, and set out in a great procession to Westminster Abbey. The Tower is open for visiting all year round, but the accomodation there is reserved for the resident community of Yeoman Warders and their families, and other Tower officials.

469
Leeds Castle, Kent
Henry visited regularly, most notably spending four days here in 1520 with Katherine of Aragon (accompanied by 4,000 courtiers!) on their way to the massive celebration in France that became known as the Field of Cloth of Gold.

470
Thornbury Castle, Thornbury, South Gloucestershire
Henry appropriated Thornbury from its disgraced owner the Duke of Buckingham, who was executed for treason at the Tower. Henry and Anne spent ten days here in 1533.

471
Oatlands Park Hotel, Weybridge, Surrey
This now privately-owned country house is built on the site of one of Henry's lost palaces, which covered around nine acres. Henry visited occasionally, and also married Catherine Howard in the chapel here.

472
Hever Castle
There are 21 bedrooms to choose from in Anne Boleyn's childhood home. The castle was also passed to Henry's fourth wife, Anne of Cleves. This stunning castle features heavily in Philippa Gregory's novel, *The Other Boleyn Girl*, that was made into the 2008 film starring Eric Bana as Henry, Scarlett Johansson as Mary Boleyn and Natalie Portman as the doomed Anne.

473
Hampton Court Palace, Surrey
Alas, Henry's private apartments containing his bedchamber are lost, pulled down to make way for the baroque palace of William and Mary. However, it's possible to stay in other locations throughout this atmospheric palace.

474
Windsor Castle, Berkshire
Henry is sleeping here permanently; he is buried with his favourite wife, Jane Seymour, in St George's Chapel. As Windsor is an occupied royal palace, staying overnight may be difficult unless by personal invitation of the royal family.

475
St James's Palace, Westminster, London
Anne Boleyn stayed here on the night after her coronation. This royal palace, which Henry later gave over for the use of his illegitimate son Henry Fitzroy, is not open to the public. Fitzroy, who for a while was Henry's first choice to inherit the throne, died here in 1536 aged only 17.

476
Cockfield Hall, Yoxford, Suffolk
A slightly looser connection to Henry, (but it's a lovely place to stay!) the King's great-niece, Lady Catherine Grey, sister of Lady Jane Grey, stayed here after her imprisonment at the Tower in the 1560s for marrying without Elizabeth I's permission. She died shortly after arriving and is buried in Yoxford Church.

Name that wife!

Try this quick-fire quiz to test your knowledge

Answers on opposite page

Identify the queen by the length of her marriage to Henry:

477
6 months

478
3 years and 6 months

479
3 years and 3 months

480
23 years and 11 months

481
2 years and 6 months

482
1 year and 4 months

Name each wife by their age, and Henry's, on their wedding day:

483
26 or 27, and 44

484
23 and 17

485
About 17, and 49

486
31 or 32, and 41

487
31 and 52

488
24 and 48

Match the motto to the wife:

489
'The most happy'

490
'To be useful in all I do'

491
'No other will but his'

492
'Bound to obey and serve'

493
'Humble and loyal'

494
'God send me well to keep'

Who was described like this by their contemporaries?

495
'No great beauty'

496
'The most beautiful creature in the world'

497
'A lady of moderate beauty, but superlative grace'

498
'So fair a lady … and so womanly a countenance'

499
'Good looking enough'

500
'Graceful, and of cheerful countenance'

477
Anne of Cleves
478
Kateryn Parr
479
Anne Boleyn
480
Katherine of Aragon
481
Catherine Howard
482
Jane Seymour
483
Jane Seymour and Henry
484
Katherine of Aragon and Henry
485
Catherine Howard and Henry
486
Anne Boleyn and Henry
487
Kateryn Parr and Henry
488
Anne of Cleves and Henry
489
Anne Boleyn
490
Kateryn Parr
491
Catherine Howard
492
Jane Seymour
493
Katherine of Aragon
494
Anne of Cleves
495
Jane Seymour
496
Katherine of Aragon
497
Catherine Howard
498
Anne of Cleves
499
Anne Boleyn
500
Kateryn Parr

Index

Credits

Cover: left to right from top: © Historic Royal Palaces; © Historic Royal Palaces; © Historic Royal Palaces; The Bridgeman Art Library (National Gallery of Art, Washington DC, USA); The Bridgeman Art Library (Private Collection); The Royal Collection © 2009 Her Majesty Queen Elizabeth II; © Historic Royal Palaces; The Royal Collection © 2009 Her Majesty Queen Elizabeth II; National Museums Liverpool (The Walker); National Museums Liverpool (The Walker); National Museums Liverpool (The Walker); By permission of the British Library (Cotton MS Augustus Ii,9); The Bridgeman Art Library (FORBES Magazine Collection, New York, USA); The Bridgeman Art Library (Private Collection); By permission of the Dean and Canons of Windsor; ©Historic Royal Palaces (Vivian Russell), © Historic Royal Palaces; The Royal Collection © 2009 Her Majesty Queen Elizabeth II; © National Portrait Gallery, London; © Rex Features; By permission of the British Library (Harl 5102 f.32); © Historic Royal Palaces; The Royal Collection © 2009 Her Majesty Queen Elizabeth II; © National Portrait Gallery, London; © Historic Royal Palaces; © Historic Royal Palaces; The Bridgeman Art Library (Private Collection/Ken Welsh); © The Board of Trustees of the Armouries; © Historic Royal Palaces; © The British Museum; The Bridgeman Art Library (© Wakefield Museums and Galleries, West Yorkshire, UK); © Historic Royal Palaces; © Historic Royal Palaces.

Main picture credits: akg-images: page 110l © Jon Arnold Images Ltd/Alamy: page 136; © The Board of Trustees of the Armouries: pages 22, 23, 24t, 24l, 25 114-115t; Ashmolean Museum, Oxford: pages 76, 90t; © Bettmann/CORBIS: page 110r; Fonds bibliothèque Méjanes, Aix-en-Provence: page 125l; Bodleian Library, University of Oxford: pages 83r, 118r; The Bridgeman Art Library: pages 16l, 116, 126r, 127l (Thyssen-Bornemisza Collection, Madrid, Spain), 17b (© Ashmolean Museum, University of Oxford, UK), 18 (National Library, St Petersburg, Russia), 20-21 and 33r (National Portrait Gallery, London, UK), 28l (Hever Castle Ltd, Kent, UK), 29 (Allen Memorial Art Museum, Oberlin College, Ohio, USA/Mrs FF Prentiss Fund), 37, 41, 146(2), and 146(4) (Kunsthistorisches Museum, Vienna, Austria), 42 and 146(5) (Louvre, Paris, France/ Giraudon), 32l, 45, 146(1) and 147l (Private Collection/© Philip Mould Ltd, London), 52 (Forbes Magazine Collection, New York, USA), 55 (National Gallery of Art, Washington DC, USA), 58 (Private Collection), 62 (Private Collection), 65b (Private Collection) 88t (Kingston Lacy, Dorset, UK/National Trust Photographic Library), 88br (Private Collection), 90b (Private Collection), 91t (© Wakefield Museums and Galleries, West Yorkshire, UK), 93r (© Corpus Christi College, Oxford, UK) 106l (Private Collection/Ken Welsh), 106-7 (Private Collection), 107r (Private Collection/The Stapleton Collection), 108 (The British Library, London, UK/ © British Library Board), 109l (Galleria degli Uffizi, Florence, Italy), 109c (Schloss Ambras, Austria), 109r (Bibliothèque des Arts Decoratifs, Paris, France/Archives Charmet), 111 (Bibliothèque Nationale, Paris, France/Lauros/ Giraudon), 114l Private Collection/ Paul Freeman, 124 and 125c (© The Berger Collection at the Denver Art Museum, USA), 132r (Private Collection), 133l (Private Collection/The Stapleton Collection); By permission of The British Library: pages 14 (Add MS 31922 f14v15), 20 (Cotton Augustus A III f35), 26b (Roy 2A XVI f63v), 69r (Harley 2278 4v), 84r (14 E VI, f208), 89 (Cotton MS Augustus Ii,9), 98 (Royal 2A XVI, f3), 139 (Royal MS 12.CVIII f4); © The British Museum: pages 15 (1852,0519.2), 86 (1854-6-28-74), 103 (1927,0721.4), 140r (P&D SL 5308.116), 141l (1892,501.1); In the collection of The Trustees of the Ninth Duke of Buccleuch's Chattels Fund: page 94r; The College of Arms: pages 26-27t, 54; Corbis page 110r; © Culture and Sport Glasgow (Museums): pages 100-101; © English Heritage Photo Library: page 68l; © The Goldsmiths' Company: page 140l; Sonia Halliday Photographs: pages 68-69; © Hamilton Kerr Institute, University of Cambridge: page 126l; Hever Castle, Kent, UK: page 145; Crown copyright: Historic Royal Palaces: pages 85t, 97; © Historic Royal Palaces: pages 27bl (Vivian Russell), 84c (Vivian Russell), 85r, 87 (Nick Guttridge), 95, 96 (Robin Forster), 98-9 (Robin Forster), 115l, 119t, 134t (Nick Guttridge), 135t (Nick Guttridge) 137; Kunsthistorisches Museum, Vienna, Austria: page 109c; Leeds Castle, Kent, UK: 135b; Littleblackpistol, 1998/Wikipedia: page 67; Musées royaux des Beaux-Arts, Brussels: pages 66-7; Courtesy of the Museum of London: pages 27bl, 70, 71; ©National Maritime Museum, Greenwich, London: page 118c; © National Portrait Gallery, London: pages 31r, 32l, 32r, 38, 46, 56, 61, 82l, 92r, 94l, 94c, 112l, 116, 118l, 125r, 127l, 128, 129c, 146(3) and 147r; National Museums Liverpool (The Walker): pages 8, 10, 16-17, 17r, 34, 133r; ©NTPL Derrick E. Witty: page 126fl; Reuters: page 48; © Rex Features: pages 118l, 119r, 120l, 120r, 121l, 121r, 122l, 122r, 123l, 123r, 129r, 130; The Royal Collection © 2009 Her Majesty Queen Elizabeth II: pages 6-7, 12r, 13, 24br, 28r, 30, 31l, 59, 60l, 60r, 72, 73, 74-5, 77, 79, 82r, 91b, 92l, 93l, 104, 114c, 126c, 127r, 129l, 134b, 138r, 138-139, 140-141; Steve Day on behalf of Salisbury Cathedral: page 112r; © Skyscan Balloon Photography (Source: English Heritage Photo Library): page 65t; David Souden: page 113; Topfoto: page 64; V&A Picture Library: pages 84l, 114r, 115r, 138l; The Warburg Institute: page 83l; Weidenfeld & Nicolson/Orion Books: pages 36, 39, 40, 43, 44, 47; By permission of the Dean and Canons of Windsor: pages 80, 132l; With permission of The Worshipful Company of Barbers, London: pages 19, 33l, 141r.

Timeline (left to right) pages 2-5: Fonds bibliothèque Méjanes, Aix-en-Provence; Kunsthistorisches Museum, Vienna, Austria/The Bridgeman Art Library; The Royal Collection © 2009 Her Majesty Queen Elizabeth II; © National Portrait Gallery, London; The Royal Collection © 2009 Her Majesty Queen Elizabeth II; The Royal Collection © 2009 Her Majesty Queen Elizabeth II; Galleria degli Uffizi, Florence, Italy/The Bridgeman Art Library, London; © HRP.

Timeline (left to right) pages 151-153: Private Collection/© Philip Mould Ltd, London/The Bridgeman Art Library; The Royal Collection © 2009 Her Majesty Queen Elizabeth II; © English Heritage Photo Library; National Gallery of Art, Washington DC, USA/The Bridgeman Art Library; Louvre, Paris, France/Giraudon/The Bridgeman Art Library; Private Collection/© Philip Mould Ltd, London/The Bridgeman Art Library; © National Portrait Gallery, London; Private Collection/ The Bridgeman Art Library; National Portrait Gallery, London, UK/The Bridgeman Art Library.

Historic Royal PALACES

Historic Royal Palaces is the independent charity that looks after the Tower of London, Hampton Court Palace, the Banqueting House, Kensington Palace and Kew Palace. We help everyone explore the story of how monarchs and people have shaped society, in some of the greatest palaces ever built.

We receive no funding from the Government or the Crown, so we depend on the support of our visitors, members, donors, volunteers and sponsors.

Published by
Historic Royal Palaces
Hampton Court Palace
Surrey
KT8 9AU

ISBN
978-1-873993-12-5

Editor **Sarah Kilby**
Pictures sourced by
Annie Heron, Louise Nash and Susan Mennell
With special thanks to
Clare Murphy
Design **Atelier Works**
Print **City Digital Ltd**

Historic Royal Palaces is a registered charity (no.1068852)

www.hrp.org.uk

1529

1532

1533

1534

Cardinal
Wolsey is
accused of
High Treason
but dies before
he can be
brought to trial

Sir Thomas
More becomes
Chancellor of
England

14 November
Henry secretly
marries Anne
Boleyn

25 January
Henry officially
marries Anne
Boleyn

23 May
Henry's 24-
year marriage
to Katherine
of Aragon is
annulled

7 September
Anne Boleyn
gives birth
to Princess
Elizabeth

November
The Act of
Supremacy
is passed,
establishing
Henry VIII as
Supreme Head
of the Church
of England

1532
Francisco Pizarro
conquers Peru and
executes Atahualpa,
the last sovereign
emperor of the Inca
Empire

1533
Ivan IV (The Terrible)
succeeds his father
as Grand Prince of
Moscow at 3-years old

1536   1537   1540   1541   1542

Henry begins
the dissolution
of the
monasteries

19 May
Anne Boleyn
is executed at
the Tower of
London

30 May
Henry marries
his third wife,
Jane Seymour

23 July
Henry Fitzroy,
the King's
illegitimate
son, dies

12 October
Jane Seymour
gives birth to
Prince Edward
at Hampton
Court

24 October
Jane Seymour
dies from
postnatal
complications

6 January
Henry marries
Anne of Cleves;
the marriage
is annulled six
months later

8 August
Henry marries
Catherine
Howard, his
fifth wife

23 June
Henry is
proclaimed
King of Ireland
and Head
of the Irish
Church

13 February
Catherine
Howard is
executed at
the Tower of
London

10 May 1537
Severe eruption of
Mount Etna

1540
Work commences
on Stirling Palace for
James V of Scotland

1541
Hungary is conquered
by the Turks and
remains a Turkish
province until 1688

1542
Abolition of Indian
slavery in Spain's
American colonies